SAMER ABU HAWWASH

Ruins and Other Poems

translated from Arabic by Huda J. Fakhreddine

 WORLD POETRY

Ruins and Other Poems
Copyright © Samer Abu Hawwash, 2025
English translation and introduction copyright © Huda J. Fakhreddine, 2025

The poem "Ruins" was originally published as *Atlal* by Al-Mutawassit in 2020.
The other poems in this book, except for "A Box of Dates on the Kitchen Table," appeared in Samer Abu Hawwash's 2024 collection, *Min al-bahr ila al-nahr* (From the River to the Sea), also published by Al-Mutawassit.

Earlier versions of the translations in this book appeared in *ArabLit*, *Asymptote*, *Literary Hub*, *Mizna*, and *Massachusetts Review*. Many thanks to the editors of these journals.

First Edition, First Printing, 2025
ISBN 978-1-954218-40-6

World Poetry Books
New York, NY
www.worldpoetrybooks.com

World Poetry titles are distributed by Asterism Books (US) and Turnaround Publisher Services (UK). Subscriptions and standing orders are available from the publisher.

Library of Congress Control Number: 2025943386

Cover image: Bashar Alhroub, *Salt Land #7* (detail), 2021, acrylic on canvas, 122 x 700 cm. Printed with the permission of the artist.

Cover design by Andrew Bourne
Typesetting by Don't Look Now
Printed in Lithuania by BALTO Print

World Poetry Books is a 501(c)(3) nonprofit and registered charity founded in 2017 in New York City and a member of the Community of Literary Magazines and Presses (CLMP).

World Poetry's publications and programs are made possible by grants from the Poetry Foundation, Hawthornden Foundation, and the New York State Council on the Arts with the support of the Office of the Governor and the New York State Legislature, and supported by an affiliation with the Humanities Institute and the Translation Program at the University of Connecticut (Storrs), as well as individual donors and our subscribers. To learn more about supporting World Poetry, please visit our website: worldpoetrybooks.com/support.

Table of Contents

Introduction — vii

Ruins
  I. The Music of Rubble — 13
  II. Out — 49
  III. A Bench Remembers — 81

It No Longer Matters If Anyone Loves Us — 103
My People — 107
The Final City — 113
From the River to the Sea — 123
We Will Lose This War — 127
A Box of Dates on the Kitchen Table — 133

Introduction

"These stones won't speak / and they won't go away." This is how Samer Abu Hawwash stands upon the ruins, as has every poet of Arabic since the beginning of time. The stones are the ruins of time, the remnants of experience and loss, and in Abu Hawwash's moment, they become signposts of exile, diaspora, languages, translation, refugeedom, and displacement.

The original landscape of Arabic poetry is the open expanse, the wavering horizon, the desert with all its layers of meaning and potential of meaning. In that landscape, the qasida, the archetypal Arabic poetic form, is rooted. It is an edifice of form, an arrangement of sound and motifs that has stood the test of time. It has also survived the narrow and flattening view of academics and scholars who often describe it as classical or old. The qasida I am referring to here defies history and all its labels, which fall short of expressing the poetic charge of this agile, versatile, and dynamic linguistic and rhetorical world with which every Arabic poetic utterance engages or contends on some level.

Every modern Arabic poetic movement has emerged from some form of engagement or dialogue with this autochthonous Arabic poem, even those that have varied on it or rejected it, as in the case of free verse and prose poetry. The ruins of the qasida have triumphed over history and continued to be the gates to poetry in Arabic.

The qasida always launches from a confrontation with time, from a reflection on ruin, a conversation with stones, traces of lost times and loved ones, the *atlal*. The poet then journeys, turns away from the site of ruin, and sets off into the desert, the inventory of meanings and images, searching for a language to break the silence, a language to reconstruct a world in place of the lost one. The poet's journey is often in search of direction or destination. The final movement of the qasida is the arrival or return home of the rejuvenated or rediscovered self, individual or collective, affirmed through the successful crossing of space and time, in the structure of poetic utterance.

In his book-length poem *Atlal* (Ruins), Abu Hawwash contends with the three movements of the qasida—the site of the ruin, the journey, and the return home—in three movements of his own. Writing in and from the moment of crisis, he keeps returning to ruins, forfeiting the journey and the hope of return and resolution, rearranging the elements of poetry in the Arabic tradition in search of closure or consolation—in a gesture, a shadow, a memory, an object.

Here, Samer Abu Hawwash, the prose poet, stands upon the poetic ruin, the stones at the threshold of the world of qasida-making. Despite his abandonment of the archetypal form, he maintains an investment in the original Arabic poetic landscape where he decides to ground his experience of loss and exile. He also stands upon the historical ruin, the catastrophe of our age, the Nakba of Palestine and its unfolding horrors. Directions in the moment of genocide are blurred and survival might only be possible in the poem.

The six poems that follow "Ruins" root themselves in monumental loss.

Even when not directly conversing with the qasida, the poems in this book maintain tension. In measured, lineated or block, prose poems, Abu Hawwash skillfully uses silences and pauses to shape meaning and build structure.

Abu Hawwash's poems are often shaped and structured through negation, denial, or protest. "My People" launches from the phrase "on a land, we were told, was not our land." The poem then accumulates negations: "We don't know how we got here"; "In a garden—not the most beautiful garden"; "We did not come from a place or a direction"; "We remember nothing . . ."; "We have no color"; "No god promised us anything . . ." The rare moments of affirmation are jolting, such as "when we die, we die a lot." The poem culminates in the last stanza with a shattering affirmation:

> My people write the names of their children
> on arms and legs, so they can find them
> later in the massacres.

In an undeniable genocide, "my people" write, gaze, touch, and hope. The string of negations that makes up a Palestinian life ends with preparations for a reunion somewhere "in the same darkness," beyond this horror, a return and an arrival, even if somewhere else beyond time.

In "From the River to the Sea," the poet abandons all tropes and renders language to its original function of creation: naming. Without verbs, the poem resists loss and dispossession by insisting on an inventory of life, of Palestinian life in the face of annihilation. In fact, the poem itself is a resounding act of defiance through what poetry does best, accounting for experience and holding it in language, guarding it from the treachery of time and its winds of erasure.

When "it no longer matters if anyone loves us" and when we know "we will lose this war," nothing remains but the poem, the witness, the triumph against time, the signpost in the wasteland of history.

—Huda J. Fakhreddine

أطلال

Ruins
(a poem in three movements)

I.
موسيقى الأنقاض

I.
The Music of Rubble

1.

لمْ يأتِ الصَّباحُ
وَلمْ أكنْ.

أفقتُ على سرابِ دَمعَةٍ،
وَكانَتِ الأرضُ مَنهوبَةً
بأشباحِ ذكرَياتٍ
تَتَلألأُ باهتَةً،
مثل شَمسٍ قَديمَةٍ مُلقاةٍ كمِعطَفٍ
أتلفَهُ الأسى
على كُرْسيٍّ مَهجورْ.

وَكانتْ صَبّارَةٌ يَتيمَةٌ
على عَتَبَةٍ مُتوَهَّمَةٍ؛
حيثُ ظلالٌ تعبرُ خِلسَةً
بين جِدارَيْن
أو بَينَ حياتَيْنِ مُعارَتَيْنِ،
وحيثُ لَمَساتٌ تَتَبَخَّرُ كلماتٍ
وشُرفاتٍ هَشَّةً وفُقَاعَاتٍ:
حتَّى تَصيرَ خِفَّةً خَالصَةً
في ميزَانِ الهَوَاءْ.

وكانتْ:
آثارُ أقْدامٍ مَمحوَّةٍ
على وسَادَةٍ بيضاءَ،
عُيُونٌ مبيضَّةٌ

1.

Morning didn't come;
I wasn't.

I awoke to the mirage of a tear.
The earth was ravished
by memory ghosts,
a dull glimmer
like an ancient sun,
like a sorrow-worn coat
thrown over
an empty chair.

An orphan cactus
stood at an imagined threshold
where shadows silently slipped
between two walls
or two borrowed lives,
where caresses faded into words,
flimsy balconies, and bubbles:
touch was nothing
but a pure lightness
in the balance of air.

And there were
effaced footprints
on the white pillow,
whitened eyes

على سِتارَةٍ مُهمَلَةٍ،
هَمَساتٌ ليلِيَّةٌ تختنقُ
على عُنقِ وَردةٍ،
آهَاتٌ تَتَرقرَقُ
على مِياهَ سِرِّيَّةٍ
لا تَزَالُ
تَنْحَدِرُ
على خَشَبٍ قَديمٍ
يَتوَجَّعهُ الشَّوقُ.

لَنْ تَنطقَ تلكَ الحِجَارَةُ،
ولَنْ تَنكفِئَ.
لكنَّ الضَّوءَ يَظلُّ يَستَرسِلُ
على النَّاقِصِ والمتَهَدِّمِ والمَأكولِ
كأنَّ ذِئباً أَبدياً يَنهشُ
ما تَبقَّى
مِن هذا الجِدَارِ
ويُعيدُ وَصلَهُ
بالعِوَاءْ.

حُلمٌ يَمحوهُ حُلمٌ
يَمحوهُمَا حُلمٌ آخَرُ.
فلا يَبقَى بعَدَئذٍ
سوى أثَرٍ أقَلَّ
مِنْ أَنْ يَمكثَ
وأكثَرَ مِنْ أَنْ يُفارِقَ،

fixed on the neglected curtain,
late-night whispers choking
on a rose's neck,
sighs quivering
in flowing waters
that continue to fall
on ancient
grief-stricken
wood.

These stones won't speak
and they won't go away,
but the light will persist, falling
on the absent, the broken, and the devoured,
as if an immortal wolf
gnaws and gnaws
at what's left
of this wall,
returning it
to the primordial howl.

A dream erased a dream
and both were erased by yet another dream.
Nothing remained
after that
but a trace,
too little to stay
too much to fade
and not enough

أو مِنْ أَنْ نَدعوَ صُورتَهُ الأخيرةَ
غَيمَةً أو حَجَراً.

في المَسَافةِ المُبَاغتَةِ
بَينَ صُعُودِ مَوجَةٍ
وهُبُوطِها
أرَى طَيْفَ وَلَدٍ يُشبهُني،
وأناديهِ: يا صَاحِبي.

حَيَاةٌ في مِرآةٍ. حَيَاةٌ مُضَاعَفَةٌ
في الأَسَفِ، في الخَشَبِ
المنْحوتِ صُوَراً وكلماتٍ،
في المَسرَّاتِ المُخَبَّأةِ.
حَيَاةٌ في لِسَانْ.

والآنَ لا نَعرِفُ
مَنْ الوَلَدُ
في صَوتِ الرَّجلِ،
في سُعَالِ الرَّجلِ،
في نَوْمِهِ الطَّويلِ؟
وَمَن الرَّجلُ
في نَظراتِ الوَلدِ،
في تَأتَأةِ الوَلدِ،
وفي خَطْوِهِ المُتلعثمِ؟

أيُّ جَسَدٍ
يَسْكنُ الآنَ هذا السَّريرَ،

for us to call it
a cloud or a stone.

In the sudden, surprising
distance between
the rise of a wave
and its fall,
I see the ghost of a child like me
and I call out to him, *my friend:*
yā saḥibī!

A life in a mirror, a life
compounded in regret,
in wood carved images and words,
in hidden pathways.
A life on the tongue.

We can't tell anymore:
who is the boy
in the man's voice,
the man's cough,
and his long slumber?
We can't tell anymore:
who is the man
in the boy's glances,
the boy's stutter,
and his stumbling steps?

Which body
haunts this bed now,

وَمَنْ يَقِفْ، ضَاحِكاً أَو صَامِتا،
عَلى الجَانِبِ الآخَرِ
مِنَ اللَيْلْ.

شيءٌ يَنهَضُ مَبتُوراً.

يَومٌ آخَرُ يَقودُ نَفْسَهُ، كَضَريرٍ،
إلى المَائِدَةِ.

عَقرَبٌ آخَرُ مَكسورٌ
يَنْبِضُ في مَكانِه
كَرَجلٍ يَضْرِبُ رَأسَهُ
بجدارٍ يَحسَبهُ بئراً، نَهراً،
مِرآة.

عَينانِ تَلهَثَانِ
فَوقَ ألبوم صُوَرٍ.
قَلبٌ يَبصقُ دَماً
مِنْ شِدَّةِ النُّبَاحْ:

في الخَريفْ،
أشْجارٌ صَديقةٌ تَزورُ الغَائِبَ
وَتَقِفُ عَارِيَةً في البُرْدْ.

خَلْفَ النَّافِذةِ ضَبابٌ مُتَذَكِّرٌ
يَتَذَكَّرْ.

and who is it that stands,
silent or smirking, there
on the other side
of the night?

Something awakens amputated.

Another day drives itself
like a blind man
to the table.

Another broken clock hand
throbs in place,
like a man banging his head
against a wall, thinking it
a well, a river,
a mirror.

Eyes panting
over a photo album,
a heart barking so hard
it spits blood.

In autumn,
the tree-friends visit the stranger
and stand there
naked in the cold.

Behind the windowpane,
the fog reminds itself
to remember.

المِرآةُ أيضاً ذِكرى.
أمْشاطٌ وأساورُ
وخَواتِمُ بلاستيكية مُلوَّنة
ومظلَّةٌ حَدْباءُ
ما زالتْ تَنْتَظِرُ الشِّتاءَ
في الزّاوِيَة.

المِرآةُ الذَّكرى
كلُّ ليلٍ تولدُ،
وتَندثرُ مع كلِّ فجرٍ؛
بينَ الوَقْتَينِ يومٌ آخَرُ
يهوي إلى عَتْمَة.

المِرآةُ المُتَذَكِّرَةُ
حَجَرُ صَوَّانٍ
يَقدَحُهُ الغياب.

في قَفْرِ هذه الغُرفَة
بَينَ كائناتٍ تَتَمَدَّدُ دونَ ظلالٍ،
بَينَ العَظاءَةِ والنَّسْرِ،
بَينَ البابِ والنّافذَةِ،
خَيطٌ واهٍ من حُروفٍ مَنسيَّةٍ
على ألسِنَةٍ مُتَحَجِّرَة؛
رَمْلٌ خَفِيٌّ يُؤَلِّفُ خَرائِطَهُ
ثمَّ يَمْحُوها.
قَبائِلُ مِنْ غُبارٍ واهِمٍ
تَبحَثُ عن الطَّريقِ المُبَدَّدةِ
في أثَرِ الغيوم.

The mirror is also a memory:
combs, bracelets,
colorful plastic rings,
and a bent umbrella
standing in the corner,
waiting for winter.

The mirror-memory,
is born every night
and every dawn
it disperses.
Between this time and that,
another day
falls into darkness.

The mirror conjured
in memory
is a flint
that absence
strikes.

In the wasteland of this room,
among the stretched out, shadowless creatures,
between the lizard and the eagle,
between the door and the window
between the faded line of an alphabet
forgotten on stone tongues,
invisible sand draws maps
and erases them,
tribes of deluded dust

الغُرْفَةُ، أيضاً،
إذ يَضرِبُها الحَنينُ:
غُرْفَتَان؛

شيءٌ يَتَرَخْزَحْ.

تُرابٌ يَهطِلُ داخِلَ الجُدْران،
حيثُ غَرقى كُثْرٌ يَعْزِفونَ،
بَيْنَ الشُّقُوقِ الأخيرَةِ،
مُوسيقَى الأنقاض.

لكنَّها لَيسَت صنعَةُ الترابِ وَحدَه،
البُرهاتُ أيضاً تَسطَعُ
مِنْ أماكِنها السَّريَّةِ
بَحْثاً عَنْ اسم
كُلِّ ما اختَفى؛
اليدُ اسمٌ وَجَدَّةٌ
اسمٌ وأُخْدُودٌ
اسمٌ وَدَمعَةٌ
تَشُقُّ بأناةٍ دَرْبَها الضَّيِّقَةِ
في أسوَدِ الهَواء.

اللِّسانُ ظَمَأٌ
والظَّهيرَةُ لافِتَةٌ مَكسورَةٌ
أو صُنْدوقُ بَريدٍ سِرِّيٍّ
لتَلويحات
لَمْ تَكتَمِل.

search for the roads
lost in the traces
of cloud.

The room, too,
when struck by nostalgia
becomes two rooms;

something shifts.

Soil rains down inside the walls
where drowned people play
through the cracks,
the music of ruin.

But it is not the craft of soil alone.
the moments also shine
from their secret places
in search of names
for all things gone.
The hand is a name and a grandmother,
a name and a ravine,
a name and a tear
slowly burrowing its path
in the black of air.

The tongue is thirst
and noon is a broken sign

صُحْبَةُ الشُّقُوقِ؛ صَبِيٌّ شَارِدٌ
في الفُصُولْ. شِتَاءٌ بِكْرٌ يُفكِّرُ
في أشْبَاهِهِ البَعِيدِينْ
فيَنْزِفُ نفْسَهُ
مِنْ سَقْفٍ مُثْخَنٍ
إلى آنِيَةٍ مُتَجعِّدةٍ
نَتَحلَّقُ حَوْلَهَا
ونَتأَمَّلُ غَيْمَةً تَعْرُجُ
قَطْرَةً بعد قَطْرَة
صَوْبَ ما بَقِيَ
مِنَ الأيَّامِ.

لا شيءَ في دُرْجِ الصَّباحْ.
إنَّهُ مَوسِمُ هِجرَةِ الرَّسائلِ
إلى شَمالِ العَناوينِ
المُبدَّدَةِ.

الوحيدُ في الغُرفَةِ
يُحَدِّقُ طَويلاً
في رَاحَةِ يَدِهِ
فلا يَرَى سوى عَيْنَيْهِ:
غريبا ليلٍ
تَحتَ شَفقٍ مَكْسورٍ
في انتِظارِ قَافلةٍ
لا تَصِلْ.

or a secret mailbox
into which unfinished gestures
drop.

Companion of chasms, a boy
wandering across the seasons. A virgin winter,
thinking of its distant equals,
bleeds through
a tired roof
into crooked pots.
We gather around
to contemplate a cloud limping
drop after drop
towards what's left
of days.

There's nothing in the drawer of the morning.
This is the season when letters migrate
to the North of lost addresses.

The lonely one in the room
Stares long into the palm of his hand
and sees nothing but his eyes:
two strangers in the night
under a subdued dusk,
waiting for a caravan
that never arrive.

2.

كَانَ الوَقتُ
وَلَمْ يَكُنْ؛

بُقعةٌ أُخرَى غَامِضَةٌ
تَسْطَعُ حَدَّ العَماءِ
على هذا الجِدَارِ
ثم تَخْتَفي؛

أنْظُرُها مِنْ بَعيد
وأَسَمِّيها حياتي.

أسماءٌ أخْرَى في الرَّماد؛

أسماءٌ رَمادٌ. أسماءُ الرَّمَادِ.
رَمادُ الأسماءِ.
أحْرفٌ مِن طينٍ.
جدَارٌ من أحرُف.
جدَارٌ شَارعٌ.
جدَارٌ مَدينَةٌ.
جدَارٌ جَبَلٌ.

جدَارٌ عَائلَة.

جدَارٌ نَحملُهُ معنا أينما حَلَلْنا
كَحقيبةٍ ثَقيلَةٍ

2.

Time was.
Time wasn't.

Another obscure spot
glows to the point
of blindness
on this wall
then disappears.

I gaze at it from afar
and call it my life.

Other names in ashes.

Ash-names,
the ash of names,
an alphabet of mud, mud-letters,
a wall of letters,
a wall-street,
a wall-city,
a wall-mountain.

A wall-family.
A family, a wall.

A wall we carry wherever we go,
like a heavy suitcase

نَفتَحُها مِنْ حينٍ لآخر،
مثلما نَفتحُ نَافذةً، بَاباً، عيناً،
عَلَّنا نَعثُرُ، صدفَةً،
في الحِجَارَةِ النَّاصِعَةِ
على نَظَراتِنا المَبَعثَرَة.

في مَدينةِ الجدرَانِ النَّاطقَةِ
كنتُ وَدَاعاً طَويلاً
يعدُّ أنفاسَهُ النَّاقصة.

كنتُ وَدَاعاً يَزدادُ
مَع كلِّ نَفسٍ،
وَنَفَساً يَنقصُ
مَع كلِّ وَداع.
وكنتُ رَملاً
يَتأمَّلُ صُورَتَهُ في المرآةِ،
كَهذهِ النَّافذةِ القَديمَةِ
التي لا تَزَالُ عَالقةً
في تَثاؤبِ قطَّةٍ
مِنْ ظَهيرَةِ شيءٍ بعيدٍ
نُسمِّيهِ البَارحَة.

هنا أو هناك،
أشياءٌ كثيرةٌ تَالفةٌ
من شدَّةِ الهجران.

that we open, every now and then,
the way we open a window,
a door, an eye,
hoping we'd find by chance
our glances scattered
on the white pebbles.

In the city
of speaking walls,
I was a long farewell,
counting the skipped breaths.

I was a farewell
rising
with each breath.
I was a breath
fading
with each farewell.
I was sand
contemplating itself in the mirror
like this old window
still stuck in a cat's yawn
since the noon of that distant thing
we call yesterday.

Here and there,
an abundance of things
ruined by
much abandon.

هنا
(بينَ اليدِ والضَّوء)
أو هناك
(بينَ العَيْنِ والنَّهْر)
عشبةٌ يابسةٌ أيضاً
تتهجَّى العَتْمَةَ؛
لو، هي الأخرى، تبكي،
لو تَستطَيعُ
طيفَ دمعةٍ فحسب.

هكذا أروي حَنيني الموجع
لهذا الجِدَار
الذي أَرَاهُ الآن
بوُضُوحِ إبرة
لكنِّي أخشى إنْ لَمسْتُهُ،
بنَظرِة
أَنْ يَخْتفي.

كلُّ شيءٍ الآنَ
على بُعْدِ نظرةٍ
أو لمسة؛

يكفي أنْ تَصْفقَ البابَ
نسمةٌ عابرةٌ
أو أنْ يَمرَّ شُعاعٌ بالخطأ
لتكتظَّ الغرفةُ، مُجدَّداً،
بالوُجُوهِ الغائبة.

Here
(between the hand and the light)
and there
(between the eye and the river),
a withered sprig
spelling out darkness.
If only it, too, could cry.
If only it could summon
the mere shadow
of a tear.

I tell this wall
of my pain and longing,
this wall facing me,
I see it as clear as a needle,
but I fear that if I touch it
with a glance,
it might disappear.

Everything now
is a touch or a glance
away.

All it takes is a breeze
to bang shut the door
or a passing light
to fall through the window
for absent faces to crowd
this room, again.

مُجدَّداً:
اليدُ المُتلعْثِمَةُ
والعينُ المُنصِتَةُ؛

يَومٌ آخَرُ يَقفزُ
على حَبْلِ الغِيابْ،
غُصْنٌ مُجعَّدٌ آخَرُ
يَتخيَّلُ خَريفاً يَتذكَّرُ
الخَريف.

كَمْ غياباً يتَّسِعُ
في هذا الكُوبِ المغبرِ
المَنسيِّ
مُنذ أرْبَعينَ عاماً
أو أكثْر
على حَافَّةِ النَّافذة؟

هذه عُشبةٌ
نَبَتَتْ بين جِدارَيْن
تروي قصَّةَ المَساءاتِ المَهدُوْرةِ
لوسادةٍ مهجُورةٍ
في خزانةٍ ميتة.

أُحَدِّقُ في جِدارٍ فحسب.
أرى طَريقاً مُوحِشةً
كضوءٍ

Again,
the stuttering hand
and the listening eye.

Another day jumps
the rope of absence,
another wrinkled branch
imagines an autumn
remembering autumn.

How many absences
can this dusty old mug,
left on the windowsill
for more than forty years,
contain?

This spear of grass
that sprouted between
two walls
narrates stories of wasted evenings
to an abandoned pillow
in a dead closet.

I stare at a wall.
I see an abandoned road,
as though it is a light

لا يَرَاهُ أحدٌ
وأَرَى ظلٍّ
يذَوبُ
في مِلْحِ التفاتة.

that nobody else sees,
and I see my shadow
melting
in the salt of every turn.

3.

في مَساءٍ بعيدٍ خفيفِ الفَراشَات،
الأبُ، ببيجامتِهِ النَّظيفةِ المقلَّمةِ،
يُشاهدُ نَشرَةَ الأخبار،
الابنُ البِكْرُ مُسْتَلْقٍ على الكنبة
مُحدِّقاً بلَمْبةٍ تُومِضُ، كبرقيَّةٍ،
على السَّقف.

النَّافذةُ كاميرا سرِّيَّةٌ
تُؤرِّخُ المشهد.

الأُمُّ: أُمَّهاتٌ.

كلُّ يدٍ كلُّ نَفَسٍ،
كلُّ تلويحةٍ كلُّ نظرة،
تطهو المساءَ
بنُعاس شَمْعَة
وتُوزِّعُهُ بالتَّساوي
على الجميع.

كلُّ كلمةٍ كلُّ هَمسَة،
تُطرِّزُ الضَّوءَ
تعويذاتٌ سرِّيَّةٌ
تطردُ الظِّلالَ من الغُرفِ،
وتُعيدُ الرِّياحَ المذعورةَ
إلى الكُهوف.

3.

In a distant evening quivering with butterflies,
the father, in his clean striped pajamas,
watches the news.
The eldest son, lying on the couch,
stares at a lightbulb
flickering on the ceiling.

The window,
a hidden camera,
logs the scene
in history.

The mother: many mothers.

Every hand, every breath,
every wave, every glance
simmers the evening
on a drowsy candle
and shares it
with everyone.

Every word, every whisper
embroiders the light.
Secret incantations
banish shadows from rooms
and send the frightened winds
to their caves.

يدٌ على سِتارَة. يدٌ سِتارةٌ.
المخملُ لا يَنطِقُ ولا يُنطِقْ:
حَرفٌ آخَرُ
مُعلَّقٌ
في هُدبِ المساءِ العاري.

يدٌ تربتُ الهَوَاءَ. يدٌ هواءٌ.
غُرفةُ كهفٍ.
مُستطيلُ شمسٍ أخرى، بعيدٍ،
يُضيءُ الغُرفةَ.

يدٌ أخرى تُزيحُ السِّتارةَ
على حياةٍ كاملةٍ
لحظةَ إقلاعِها.

لا أَحَدَ في البيت؛
فقط، طفلٌ في السَّابعةِ
يَستمتعُ بالبُرودةِ
على المصطبةِ،
مُنشغلاً بتخيُّلِ حيواناتٍ خُرافيةٍ
على سَطحِ بَلاطةٍ قديمة.

ينظرُ، فجأةً،
بِعينَينِ واضحَتَيْنِ،
يراني
على بُعدِ أربعينَ عاماً
ويَحزن.

A hand on a curtain; it is a curtain.
Velvet neither speaks nor is it spoken—
another letter hangs
on the eyelids of the naked evening.

A hand caresses the air; it is air.
A room, a cave.
The rectangle of another distant sun
illuminates the room.

Another hand pulls back the curtain
on a whole life
at the moment of departure.

No one is home;
only a seven-year-old child
enjoying the cool
on the porch
imagining mythical creatures
on the surface of old tiles.

Suddenly, he looks up
with clear eyes,
sees me
from forty years away
and grows sad.

لو تستطيعُ تلكَ الطَّاولةُ
أنْ تُسافرَ في الزَّمَن،
لجاءتْ، إذنْ، بالضَّحكِ
بالبُخارِ الصَّاعدِ من الحساءْ،
بالأيدي الكثيرةِ
التي تُجري أحاديثَ عابرةً
في غَفْلةٍ منَ المساءِ
وأهلِهِ الضَّائعين.

الطَّريقُ
مِنَ البيتِ إلى المدرَسة،
مِنَ البيتِ إلى الجَدَّة،
مِنَ البيتِ إلى السَّاحَة،
مِنَ البيتِ إلى العالم،
لشدَّة ألفَتِه
يبدو الآنَ
رِوَاقاً صغيراً
بينَ غُرفتين.

أمُرُّ بهمْ
مثلما تمرُّ ريحٌ بَطيئةٌ
على حَقلٍ مُقفرٍ،
أجدهمْ جَالسينَ
على مَداخِلِ بيُوتٍ ودَكاكينَ،
يَرفعونَ رؤوسَهُمْ، وينظرونَ إليَّ
ولا يقولُونَ شيئاً.

If only that table
could travel through time,
it would have brought back laughter,
the rising steam of soup,
and the many hands
engaged in fleeting conversations,
unnoticed by the evening
and its lost dwellers.

The road
from home to school,
from home to grandmother's
from home to the square,
from home to the world—
so familiar,
it now seems
like a narrow corridor
between two rooms.

I pass them by
like a slow wind
over a barren field.
I find them seated
in the doorways of houses and shops.
They lift their heads to look at me—
but say nothing.

فَجأةَ عَتْمَةٌ
تُشبهُ الشِّتاءَ
تمحو النَّظراتَ
عن الوُجُوه.

أيّتها الشَّقيقاتُ
أنا دُميتُكُنَّ الشَّقراءُ الجديدة،
ألبِسنَني الفساتينَ الزَّاهية،
ودَعَنَني أمشي
مُتعثراً بالكعبِ العالي
إلى ضَحِكاتِكُنَّ الشَّاهقة.

بابٌ على الغُبار. بابُ غُبارٍ.
وإنّي الآنَ هنا
طريدُ جدرانٍ حَبيسِ ضوءٍ
يَظلُّ يَتمدَّدُ إلى الدَّاخل؛
حيثُ لا زَمَنَ يكفي
لاستعادةِ بُرهَة،
وحيثُ بُرهَةٌ تكفي
ليقفَ كلُّ شيء
مثلما كلُّ شيء كان
ومثلما كلُّ شيء
يوماً
لنْ يكون.

Suddenly, a darkness
like winter
wipes the looks
off their faces.

Dear sisters,
I am your new blond doll.
Dress me in your bright dresses
and let me stumble in high heels
toward your steep laughter.

A door onto dust. A door of dust.
And here I am now,
a fugitive of walls, a prisoner of a light
that keeps stretching inward
where no time is enough
to reclaim a moment
and where a moment is enough
for everything to stand still
as everything once was
and as everything
will one day
never be.

هنا، أخيراً، حيثُ تتوقَّفُ الأسماءُ:
حيثُ الكَلِماتُ، طَواعِيةً، تَعودُ
إلى لثغاتِها الأولى،
حيثُ لا شيءَ ينمو أو يَذوي،
يَكتملُ أو يَنقصُ،
أنظرُ مِنَ النَّافذةِ
فأرى في الأفقِ البعيدِ
كومةَ حِجارةٍ
تصُنعَ شخصاً
يتلاشى في الظَّلامْ.

أمدُّ يدي
إلى آخرِ الهَوَاء
وأناديه:
يا صاحِبي.

Here, at last, where names stop,
where words willingly return
to their first lisps,
where nothing grows or withers,
completes or diminishes,
I look out the window
and see on the distant horizon
a heap of stones
in the shape of a person
fading in the dark.

I reach my hand
toward the edge of air
and call out to my friend:
yā saḥibī!

II.
في عَرَاءٍ

**II.
Out**

1.

إنكَ تسبحُ
في عَراءٍ
خاصٍّ
مِنْ
صُنعِكَ

على ارْتفاعٍ
ما
مِنْ وَجهِكَ

مِنْ تُربةٍ
تنهالُ
كذكرى بَعيدةٍ،
على مَقرُبةٍ شَديدةٍ
مِن
أحلامِكَ.

ألمٌّ ما،
غيرَ مُحدَّدٍ
كالصَّباح

كَكلِّ صباح

كَكلِّ شيءٍ،
ههنا،
مُسْتقيمٍ

1.

You swim out
into an open
expanse
of your own
making

a few inches
above your face

above the soil
raining down
like a distant memory,
so close
to your dreams.

An uncertain pain
like morning

like every morning

like everything here,
straight
and turned
upside down.

بالمقلوب.
ألمٌ ما،
لكنَّهُ هنا أيضاً.

تَعرفُ ذلكَ
مِن رَعْشَةٍ مُفاجئةٍ
تَتَسَلَّلُ إلى يَدَيك؛

تَقِفُ مُرتجفاً
مِنَ الدَّاخلِ
كشَجرةٍ
في يَبَاس.

العَناوينُ تَفقدُ وِجْهَتَها، فلا يَعودُ فَرقٌ بينَ اللَّمسةِ والدَّمعة، بينَ الخطوةِ الأولى والصَّمتِ الأخير، بينَ اليوم وظلِّه. قَدَمٌ تَدوسُ، بالخطأ، عُشبةً يابسةً، فتتداعى الغُرَف، والبيتُ يَفقدُ توازنُه، ويَرتدُّ خُطواتٍ خَريفيةً إلى الـوراء. حَصوةٌ واحدةٌ تَفصِلُنا عن الأمس، لكنَّ البحيرةَ التي انتظرْناها طَويلاً جدّاً لَم تَعدْ أكثرَ مِن ضَبابٍ يَتمدَّدُ، كَرقصةٍ بَطيئةٍ، على جَانبَيْ حَياةٍ،
لَمْ تَعُدْ هنا.

ضَوءٌ
يَنْبِضُ
داخلَ
حَجَر

كالأسف

A pain somewhere,
but also here.

You know it
from the sudden shiver
that takes over your hands.

You stand quivering
on the inside
like a withering tree.

The addresses lose their direction. No difference between a
touch and a tear, between the first step and the final silence,
between the day and its shadow. A foot mistakenly steps on a dry blade of grass, the rooms collapse, the
house loses its balance, autumn retreats a few steps backward. One pebble separates us from yesterday, but the lake
we waited for so long has become nothing more than fog
spreading like a slow dance on the edges of a life
that is no longer here.

Light
throbs
in a stone,

like remorse,

كشجرةٍ، كلَّما نامتْ،
أبصرتْ جُذُورَها
حَشداً
مِنَ
الأفواهِ
الجائعة.

حِجارةٌ، بلا نهاية،
تَسقطُ
في هِواءٍ معطَّلٍ
في مِرآةِ
بِئرٍ.

ضَوءٌ يَتيمٌ
لا يَزالُ يتسلَّقُ
سَريرَ رَجلٍ
لَمْ يَعُدْ هنا؛

فَرَاغٌ جَليدِيّ
في موضع السَّريرْ
حَيثُ لا شيءَ،
بَعدَ الآن،
يَعبر.

البيتُ، في الذِّكرى،
شخصٌ من ظلالٍ
أو حشدُ عصافيرَ
يَصنعُ اسماً

like a tree

that sees its roots

in a dream,

a throng

of hungry maws.

Stones endlessly

falling

into the stalled air

in the mirror of

a well.

An orphan light

still climbing

the bed of a man

who is no longer there.

An icy void

in the spot where the bed was,

where nothing

after now

will pass.

The house in memory

is a figure of shadows

or a flock of birds

tracing a name

على ضبابِ نافذةٍ
ثمَّ يتلاشى في الهَوَاءِ
كأُغْنيَّةٍ
في رَوْعِ طِفل.

كأنني آتٍ مِن بُعدٍ آخَرَ، أسْتَعيرُ حَياةً صَباحيَّةً، أَدْخُلُ بِهَا المَطبخ. على مَسَافةِ أربَعينَ عَاماً مِنْ تلكَ الغُرف، أَتَلفَّتُ بحثاً عَن وجهٍ أَعْرِفُهُ؛ صَوْتٌ يُنادي اسْماً، يَظلُّ مُعَلَّقاً في الهَوَاءِ. المياهُ رَاكدةٌ في الكُوب. اللَّيلُ مُتواصِلٌ على سَطحِ القَهوَةِ. الصَّوتُ يَجيءُ وَيرحَلُ كمطرٍ يَظلُّ يُغمضُ، ويَفتحُ، عينَيْه.

وجهُكَ هذا
الذي يُحاولُ، عَبَثَاً،
أنْ يَقولَ شيئاً ما؛
لا فَرقَ، الآنَ، بينَهُ
وبينَ الغُبارِ المُتكوَّمِ
كحشدٍ غامِضٍ
يَتقدَّمُ
في سَنتيمترٍ واحدٍ
مِنَ العَتْمَة.

on the fogged window.
It vanishes in the air
the way a tune disperses
in the terror of a child.

It's as if I come from another dimension. I borrow a morning life and take it with me into the kitchen. At a distance of forty years from those rooms, I turn around searching for a face I know. A voice calls a name and remains hanging in the air. The water is still in the cup. The night expands on the surface of coffee. The voice comes and goes like rain, constantly closing and opening its eyes.

Your face
that tries in vain
to say something
is no different
from a pile of dust,
like a mysterious crowd
advancing
within a centimeter
of darkness.

2.

قُلْ شيئاً عن الأسف؛
شَمسٌ سَاطعةٌ
بما فيهِ الكفايةُ
على البلاط،
مِرآة تَتَشظَّى،
رجلٌ
يَجفُّ
في
عَيْنَيه.

أو قُلْ
لحظةً عاديَّةً جدّاً؛
يَدٌ، مثلاً، في الظَّهيرة،
في طَقْسٍ
غيرِ قابلٍ للقياس،
تمتدُّ عموديَّةً
مِن نَافذةِ سَيَّارةٍ مُسرعةٍ
نَحْوَ عَدمٍ واضحٍ
وغيرِ قابلٍ، هو الآخرُ،
للقِياس.

تماماً كحقلٍ،
تلكَ اللَّمساتُ الصَّغيرةُ
تَبحثُ عن أيديها الضَّائعةِ
في بُرهَةٍ
تَتَذكَّر.

2.

Say something about sorrow:
a sun shining
just enough
on the tiles,
a mirror
shattered,
a man
shriveled
in his own
eyes.

Or say:
A very ordinary moment,
for example a hand
at noontime
and the weather
difficult to discern,
stretches horizontally
from the window of a car
rushing
toward a clear unknown,
that is also
difficult to discern.

Just like a meadow,
these blind caresses
search for their lost hands
in a moment
that remembers.

أجلسُ هنا، على كُرسيٍّ مِنْ صُنعِ ذاتي. شجرةُ الصُّورِ نُجومٌ تَهطُلُ مِنْ سَقفِ الغرفةِ، حيثُ جدارٌ آخرُ، حيثُ أُطيلُ النَّظرَ نَحوَ ما يَبـدو أَثراً لِحَيـاةٍ تركضُ في زاروب. أركضُ خلفَه، وَنَلتقي عندَ نُقطةٍ ذائبةٍ، على بُعْدِ يَوم واحدٍ مِنَ الحُبِّ أو الأسفِ أو مِنْ تلكَ النَّظَرات التي صارتْ أثراً باهتاً على جِدار.

واقفٌ
على بُعْدِ فكرةٍ
صغيرةٍ جدَّاً
كَشُرفةٍ
لا أعرفُ
مِنْ أيَّةِ حياةٍ
سَابقة

كضوءِ سيَّارةٍ
يَظلُّ يَعبرُ
تَحتَ قَمرٍ مُكتملِ
اليباس.

أيُّها الذينَ
ما
عادُوا
هنا
أو
هناك.

أو لِمَ لا أقولُ:
أيُّها الأشخاصُ
أيَّتها الأشياءُ،

I sit here in a chair I've fashioned out of myself. A tree of pictures. Stars falling from the ceiling of the room where another wall stands, where I gaze long at what seems like a trace of a life running through the alley. I run after it and we meet at a melting point, one day away from love or regret or those glances that have become a mark faded on a wall.

Standing
at the distance
of a passing thought,
like a balcony
from some past life—
I am not sure which.

Like the headlights of a car
that keeps passing
under a fully
shriveled
moon.

O you who
are no longer
here
or
there.

Or why don't I just say:
O you, people,

أيُّها الأشخاصُ
في الأشياء
أيَّتها الأشياءُ
في الأشخاص.
أيُّها الأشخاصُ الأشياءُ
أيَّتها الأشياءُ الأشخاص.
بُرْهَةٌ طويلةٌ
يأتي بها الصَّباحُ عُنوةً
على سَطْحِ حياةٍ واحدةٍ
سَعيدةٍ
لِواحدٍ مِنَّا
فحسب.

في رأسي
فحسبُ
هذه السِّتارةُ المفتُوحةُ
كَبَابْ

في رأسي
فحسبُ
هذا الضَّحكُ
الغارقُ
في حَنينهِ
المُضحِك.

صحراءٌ أبديَّةٌ في راحةِ يدٍ. أمامَ هذه المرآةِ، وجهي، مُجدَّداً، يُفلتُ منِّي. المدينةُ حيلةٌ بارعةٌ أضاعتْ ساحرها في الشَّتاتِ العظيم. النهارُ لطخةٌ حمراءُ، تشتعلُ، كوردةٍ، على جدار. ولدُ

you things,

you people in things,

you things in people.

you people-things,

you thing-people.

A long moment

that the morning forcibly brings

to the surface of life,

a happy one—

a happiness enough for only

one of us.

Only in my head

does this curtain open

like a door.

Only

in my head

this laughter

drowns

in laughable

yearning.

An eternal desert in the palm of a hand. In front of the mirror, my face escapes me again. The city is a clever trick that has lost its magician in the great diaspora. Day is a red stain that burns like a rose on the wall. A boy runs naked toward

يركضُ، عارياً، نحو المطر. غيمةٌ سرِّيَّةٌ تجمعُ كلَّ الشِّتاءاتِ الماضيةِ، والآتيةِ، في قطرةٍ واحدة.

الساحرُ،
أيضاً،
ابتلعتْهُ
القُبَّعةُ
المُخبَّأةُ
في
كُمِّ
أحلامِهِ
الضَّيِّقِ.

لا أحَدَ يَعرفُ
أنَّها يَدُهُ
تلك الممتدَّةُ
مِنَ الجِدَارِ
كَصرخةٍ
في ذُهُول.

لا أحَدَ يَراني/ يَراكَ
واقفاً
على رَصيفٍ مُرتَجَلٍ
من هَوَاءٍ وعُيُونٍ
بيدٍ لا تَسمَعُ
وقلبٍ لا يَرَى
أطرقُ/ تطرقُ
باباً

the rain. A secret cloud collects all the winters, those gone and those yet to come, in a single drop.

The magician,

he too,

was swallowed

by the hat

hidden in

his dream's

tight sleeve.

Nobody knows

that it is his hand

that stretches

from the wall

like one shouting

in awe.

No one sees me / sees you

standing on a pavement

improvised of air and eyes.

With a deaf hand

and a blind heart,

I knock / you knock

on a door

يُبدِّلُ جِلْدَهُ
مع كلِّ شُعَاع.

لا يَهمُّ
لا يَهمُّ حقًّا:

على أَحَدِنا، في النِّهايةِ،
أنْ يَحملَ هذا المِعْوَلَ
لننقلَ، مِنْ هنا
إلى هناك،
جَبلَ النَّظراتِ هذا
الذي يَقطعُ أعمارَنا
إلى نِصْفَين.

that changes its skin
with every ray of light.

It doesn't matter.
It really doesn't.

One of us must eventually
pick up a shovel
so we can move
from here to there
this mountain of glances
that cuts our lives
in half.

3.

قُلْ شيئاً عن العُزْلَة؛
عُصفُورٌ بلا ذِكْرى
أو سَماءْ
يَقفُ صَامِتاً تماماً
على رَأسِ شَارعٍ
بَعدَ مُنتصَفِ ليلٍ
ينتظرُ حَافِلةً أُخرى
يَعرِفُ أنَّها لنْ تَصِلْ
لأنَّها لم تصل
لأنَّها لن تصل
ككلِّ شيءٍ
آخر.

أريدُ شيئاً عاديًّا،
شيئاً سخيفاً،
كالشَّيءِ السَّخيفِ نفسِهِ
الذي ظَلَلْتُ
لا أبحثُ عنه
طوالَ حيواتي
السَّابقة.

أخافُ، الآنَ،
لو أعطيتُهُ اسماً
أن يضيعَ
مرَّةً أُخرى.
أخافُ،

3.

Say something about isolation:

a bird without memory

or a sky

stands completely silent

at a street corner

after midnight

waiting for another bus

he knows won't come

because it hasn't arrived yet

and because,

like all other things,

it never will.

I want something ordinary.

Something silly

like that same silly thing

I spent my past lives

not looking for.

I worry now

that if I gave it a name

I might lose it

again.

I worry

that if I open

لو فَتحْتُ عينَيَّ
أن أرى.

المفرشُ الفاخرُ
وضعتُهُ على الطَّاولةِ
الكُؤُوسُ ملأتُها
بما تبقَّى من حنين
الهواءُ أفرَغْتُهُ
من كلِّ الكلماتِ المُغبَرَّة

ولم يَأتِ أبي.

أبي
منذُ أربعينَ عاماً
يقفُ
في العَتْمَةِ نفسِها
أمامَ البابِ نفسه
ومِنْ عينَيْهِ فقط
تنهمرُ
على المفاتيح
كلُّ الظِّلالِ المَنسِيَّةِ
مثلما تنهمرُ
على الظِّلالْ
كلُّ المفاتيحِ الضَّائعة.

أريدُ أنْ أقولَ شيئاً لكلِّ الأشياءِ التي ضَاعتْ قبلَ أنْ أعرفَ، قبلَ تلك الخرائطِ اللامَرئيَّةِ على جِلدِي؛ ثمَّة أساطيلُ من اللَّمساتِ تَجوبُ هذه المياهَ المُعْتِمَةَ، ثمَّة رحَّالةٌ بلا عُيُون، يَقفونَ على

my eyes
I might see.

I laid the fancy spread
on the table. I filled the cups
with what's left of longing
and I emptied the air
of all the dusty words.

Still, my father didn't come.

My father has stood
in the same darkness
for forty years,
before the same door,
and from his eyes alone
all forgotten shadows
pour onto the keys,
just as all lost keys
pour onto the shadows.

I want to say something to all the things that were lost
before I realized it, before these invisible maps appeared
on my skin. There are fleets of caresses haunting these
dark waters. There are travelers without eyes, standing
at the edge of the hook on which my father hangs his

طَرَف المشجَب، حيثُ يُعلِّق أبي قميصَهُ الأبديَّ، حيثُ عُشبةٌ لا تبدأُ ولا تنتهي، تتكاثرُ فيها الأسماءُ، كالأسماكِ، كالشُّعوبِ التي سَقطتْ، من يدِ أُمِّي، على مُشمَّعِ الطَّاولة.

بُقعةٌ سوداءُ غامضةٌ
على وَجهِ الشِّتاء
أُغنيَّةٌ شعبيَّةٌ
تَسرِدُ حياتي
بكلماتٍ رديئةٍ،
لائقةٍ على الأرجح،
وغير مُتذكَّرة.
أَحدُهُمْ قَبلي
كانَ يَتخيَّلُ المَطَرَ
وهو يَبتعدُ
كَسَاعِي بريدٍ
على دَرَّاجةٍ هوائيَّةٍ سوداءَ.

أمامَ هذا الجِدارِ
ماذا تفعلُ العَينانِ النَّازفتانِ
سوى أن تَرتَفِعا مُجدَّداً
مع الدُّخانِ المُرتفِعْ.
في الشَّارع،
أَستوقِفُ غريباً
يُشبهُني تماماً،
نَنظرُ، بصمتٍ فارغٍ،
إلى واحِدنا الآخرِ،

eternal shirt, where a spear of grass that neither begins nor ends multiplies with names, like fish, like the peoples that fell from my mother's hand
onto the tablecloth.

A mysterious black stain

on the face of winter,

a folk song

narrating my life

with sappy words,

probably fitting

and easy to forget.

Someone before me

imagined the rain

drifting away

like a mailman

on a black bicycle.

In front of this wall,

what can the bleeding eyes do

but rise again

with the rising smoke?

In the street,

I stop a stranger

who looks exactly like me.

We gaze in empty silence

ثم نَستأنفُ
غِيابَنَا الفَادِح.

مواسمُ كهذه
تبدأُ دوماً
لكنَّها لا تَعرفُ
أنْ تنتهيَ.

وداعاً
يا
كُلُّ
ما/مَنْ
أضعتُ
صُورتَهَ.

عارياً تماماً
مِنْ أَساطيرِ الغُرفةِ
وأوهامِ النَّافذة
لم يبقَ لي
سوى هذا اللَّيلِ الضَّريرِ
يَتحسَّسُ وجهي
بأصابعه الغَائِبَة؛
ذلك الذُّهولُ الأبديّ
أمامَ لطخةٍ
تَرَكَتْهَا يدٌ
على زُجَاج.

at one another
then resume
our horrific absence.

Seasons like these
always begin
but never know
how to end.

Farewell
to all those
people and things
whose images
I have lost.

Completely stripped
of the room's myths
and the window's illusions,
nothing remains for me
but this blind night,
caressing my face
with its absent fingers
and that eternal bewilderment
before a smudge
left by a hand
on the glass.

كَمْ ضبابٍ
قلناهُ دونَ قَصْد،
أو بقَصْدٍ باهتٍ،
كهذهِ الوُجُوهِ
التي تظلُّ تظهرُ
وتختفي
كمدينةٍ نُسِيَتْ
خلفَ بَحْر.

أقفُ مُعدَماً على بابِ السَهرة. القمرُ كذبةٌ أخرى. والعَتبةُ بابٌ
دوَّارٌ، ليس إلَّا. لا ثأرَ لي مع هذا الغُروب وكائناتِهِ الغريبة.
ولا أعوِّل على الكلماتِ، لتُحدِثَ شيئاً آخرَ في هذه الشَّرايين.
ولذلك أكتفي بالصَّمتِ
بينما أُقلِّبُ، مع الغبارِ، صُورةً واحدةً، تتمدَّدُ في البَياضْ.

هنا،
في الجانبِ الآخرِ
من المِرْآة،
بياضٌ ينزفُ أَشْخاصَهُ،
هُنيهاتٌ تتضعضع
لمساءٍ آخَرَ،
عُيُونٌ تتسلَّقُ الجُدران
فتتناثرُ حجارةً
مُنطفِئةً
في الحُقُول.

How much fog
have we spoken unintentionally,
or with faint intent,
like these faces
that keep appearing
and disappearing,
a city forgotten
behind a sea.

I stand destitute at the door of the evening get-together.
The moon is just another lie, and the threshold, nothing but
a revolving door. I have no vendetta against this sunset and
its strange creatures, nor do I rely on words to stir up some-
thing different in these veins. And so, I settle for silence
while I turn over, in the dust,
a single image stretching into whiteness.

Here,
on the other side
of the mirror,
a whiteness bleeds out its figures,
moments collapse
into another evening,
eyes climb the walls
only to scatter as
stones extinguished
in the fields.

هنا،
على هذا السَّقْف،
فراشةٌ أُخرى تسقُط
من اللُّغة،
نجمةٌ أُخرى
تُصبحُ حَجَراً عَارياً
يَنبضُ
وحدَهُ
في الظَّلام.

Here,

on this ceiling,

another butterfly falls

from language,

another star

becomes a bare stone,

pulsing

alone

in the dark.

III.
مقعدٌ يتذكَّرُ

III.
A Bench Remembers

وراءَ الأنفاسِ المُهمَلَة
في الشُّقُوق
خريفٌ ينسدِلُ بِبُطء
من شُقُوقِ سقفٍ آخر
يُعاوِدُ البكاء
بلا سببٍ؛

عُيُون تجفُّ
على سَتَائِرَ
لم تعدْ هنا.

مساءٌ مُتعَبٌ في الصُّور.

شمسٌ صغيرة
تُولَدُ بعدَ مُنتصفِ ليلٍ
ليسَ لأحد،
منديلٌ قديمٌ
تطويهِ الأُمُّ بحذَر
وتضعُهُ بخُشُوع
على وسادةِ رجلٍ
من أسفٍ خالصٍ
وتنهُّداتٍ
وأنواع أُخرى،
غيرِ مَرئيَّة،
من الصَّمت.

مياهٌ غزيرةٌ في الأرق.

Behind the breaths

neglected in the cracks,

Autumn slowly descends.

From the cracks in another ceiling,

it returns to cry

without reason.

Eyes dry

on curtains

that are no longer there.

An evening

weary in pictures,

a small sun

born after a midnight

that belongs to no one,

an old handkerchief

carefully folded by the mother

and placed reverently

on the pillow of a man

made of sighs and regret,

and other invisible

forms of silence.

Waters gush in insomnia.

تربةٌ معجونةٌ بالحَصَى
حشائشُ يابسةٌ
وكلماتٌ تنجرفُ
من مساءٍ لآخر
ومن فمٍ لعَين
بين أرصفةٍ بَادَتْ
من كثرةِ النِّسيان
لكنَّها ظلَّتْ هنا
كنوافذَ تُومضِ
في عَتْمةٍ شاخصَة.

منذُ أربعين عاماً
هذه المسبحةُ المُتدلِّيةُ كَموجةٍ
من مِسمارٍ صَدِئٍ
على جِدارٍ مُزدحِمٍ
بالسَّاعات:

حبَّاتُها السُّود
عُيُونٌ بلا ضَوء
تحرسُ أشباهَ النَّائمين
وأولئكَ الذين انفرطَت
أسماؤُهم،
منهُم،
في الهَوَاء.

هواءٌ، ومع ذلك
لا شيءَ يتحرَّك
في الأشجار.

Soil mixed with pebbles,

dry grass,

and words that drift

from one evening to another,

from mouth to eye,

on sidewalks

faded in forgetfulness.

But they, the words, remain here

like windows flickering

in the unwavering dark.

For forty years,

these prayer beads have hung

like a wave on a rusty nail

on a wall crowded with clocks.

The black beads

are eyes without light,

guarding the shadows of sleepers

and those whose names

have unraveled

from them and scattered

in the air.

A breeze

but still nothing

moves in the trees.

رجلٌ على مقعدٍ،
هو الآخرُ لا يتحرَّكُ.

ذاكرةٌ تحاولُ أن تتذكَّرَ.

عَينانِ تسيلانِ إلى الدَّاخل.

كلماتٌ لا تُقال.

في الصُّورِ الميتة،
شيءٌ يتألَّم بوُضُوح
لكنَّنا لا نراهُ.

ما الفرقُ، إذنْ،
إن كنَّا انتقلْنا حقَّاً
مِنْ مساءٍ إلى آخرَ
أو مِنْ مكانٍ
إلى جُرحٍ؟

ما الفرقُ
إن كنَّا لم نتقدَّم
طوالَ أربعينَ عاماً
إلَّا بمقدارِ لمسةٍ
أو ذرَّةِ غُبار
كنَّا نعرفُ، طوالَ الوقت،
أنَّها كانتْ هنا؟

A man on a bench.
He too is still.

A memory
attempting to remember.

Eyes that flow inward.

Unsaid words.

In the dead photos
something clearly suffers.
We do not see it.

What difference does it make
if we truly survive
from one evening to another,
or from a place
to a wound?

What difference does it make
if we have not progressed
for forty years
except by a touch
or a speck of dust
that we knew, all along,
was here?

الصَّيفُ كلمةٌ.
واللَّمسة.

الغُرفُ، في النِّهايةِ، ليستِ الجُدران
لأنَّنا مهما حاوَلنا
لا نجدُ طريقة
لنجمعَ، في كلمةٍ واحدةٍ،
الظِّلالَ والأنفاسَ
والمياهَ السِّرِّيَّة
التي ظلَّتْ تتدفَّق
بين حَيَاتَيْنِ مَهدورَتَيْن.

الكلماتُ التي لم تَقُلْ شيئاً
لا تقولُ شيئاً الآنَ أيضاً.

أصواتٌ مُبهَمَة
كَلَيلٍ يتركُ لمسةً خفيفة
على وجهكَ،
على كتفكَ،
على المكانِ النَّائي
من روحِكَ.

رحيلٌ يحدثُ في لحظتِهِ.
الصُّورُ التي فارقَتْ
هي أيضاً الصُّورُ التي بقيَتْ؛
أقفُ وحيداً
في نهايةِ رواقٍ سرِّيٍّ

Summer is a word.
The touch, too.

The rooms, in the end, are not walls,
because no matter how hard we try,
we can't find a way to gather
in a single word
the shadows, the breaths,
and the secret waters
that continue to flow
between two wasted lives.

The words that said nothing before
still say nothing now.

Dull voices
like a night that leaves
a light touch
on your face,
on your shoulder,
on that distant spot
in your soul.

A separation that happens in the moment.
The images that faded
are also the images that stayed.
I stand alone

حيثُ بابٌ لا يتَّسع
لكلِّ هذا الصَّمت،
حيثُ الأيدي ظلالٌ صخريَّة
في بُرهَةِ وداعٍ طويل.

يدٌ تنسى نفسَها على النَّافذة
تصيرُ، في الذِّكرى، غيمة.
يدٌ تصيرُ غُباراً غيرَ مَرئيّ
على مقبض الباب،
على الطَّاولة.
الصُّورةُ على مقربةٍ شديدةٍ
من عينَيْكَ
تمحو بعضَها؛

موسيقى تصويريَّة لنسيان
نسيَ
أن يُنسى.

ليلاً،
في حجرةِ الأمس،
أتنفَّسُ بُرهَات
من حياةٍ،
ما زالَ غيابُها
يتضاعفُ
في الهَوَاء؛

يدي، في هذه العَتْمَة،
تُحاوِل أن ترى.

at the end of a secret hallway
where the door is not wide enough
for all the silence there,
where the arms are stone shadows
in a moment of long farewell.

A hand that forgets itself in the window
becomes, in memory, a cloud.
A hand becomes invisible dust
on the doorknob,
on the table.
The image, very close
against your eyes,
erases itself.

A soundtrack for a forgetting
that forgot
to be forgotten.

At night,
in the room of yesterday,
I breathe moments
from a life
whose absence
keeps multiplying
in the air.

My hand, in this darkness,
tries to see.

يتامى ضَوء،
نقفُ منتظرِين
كلَّ ما لا يَصِل،
ما لم يَصِلْ يوماً؛

كلماتٌ شحيحةٌ
تسقطُ من جُيُوبِنا
بينما نقطعُ الأيَّام
إلى شجرةِ البداية:
بيتٌ، شارعٌ، مدينةٌ،
بابٌ، نافذةٌ، ستارةٌ،
يدٌ، عينٌ، قلبٌ،
جدارٌ، لمسةٌ،
قفرٌ:

كلماتٌ حَصى على الطَّاولة؛
عُيُوننا التي
ما زالتْ،
من بعيدٍ،
تُحدِّقُ بنا.

جارحٌ هذا الهَوَاء
جارحٌ وأليفٌ، ويكادُ، لبرهَة،
أنْ يكونَ حقيقيّاً
كغُرُوبٍ في بيتٍ بعيد
كالكنبَاتِ العجائز
وقد شُغِلَت
بأصحابِها الغائبِين

Orphans of light,
we stand waiting
for all that hasn't arrived,
for all that never will.

Meager words
fall out of our pockets
as we cross the days
toward the tree of beginning:
a house, a street, a city,
a door, a window, a curtain,
a hand, an eye, a heart,
a wall, a touch.
Desolation:

word-pebbles on the table,
and our eyes,
still, from afar,
stare back at us.

This air is sharp,
sharp and familiar, and for a moment,
it almost feels real—
like a sunset in a distant house,
like old couches
preoccupied
with their absent owners,
like something

كشيءٍ
يريدُ أن يُلمَس
كلمسةٍ
تُريدُ أن تكونَ شيئاً.

كلماتٌ ضَالَّةٌ تتشبَّثُ بالحجارةِ؛
يَراعاتٌ بلا ضوء
تنحتُ عَتْمَة هذا النَّهار
ثمَّ تسقطُ
كالنَّظراتِ القديمةِ
التي تظلُّ تسقطُ
في فراغِ حجرةٍ مليئةٍ
بمقعدٍ واحدٍ
للذِّكرى فحسب.

مع ذلك، أحياناً
شجرةٌ وحيدةٌ
تضيءُ شارعاً
مثلما داخلَ العين
صخبُ الظِّلالِ الغائبة؛
ومضٌ غامضٌ ينبضُ
بما هو مُتذكِّر.

نتسلَّقُ الكلمات
إلى مُدنٍ غارقةٍ
في مياهٍ لم تصلْ.

that longs to be touched,
like a touch
longing to be something.

Lost words cling to stones.
Fireflies without light
carve the darkness of this day,
then fall
like old glances
falling
into the emptiness of a room
filled only
with a chair
for memory alone.

And yet, sometimes,
a lonely tree
illuminates a street,
just as within the eye,
absent shadows clamor,
a mysterious glimmer throbs
with something remembered.

We climb words
to cities submerged
in waters that haven't yet arrived.

نتسلَّقُ الغُرفَ إلى الكلمات
التي نحسبُها أبواباً؛
نقفُ طويلاً أمامَ المفارقة؛
أحدُنا يقولُ: "بابٌ"
فيتحجَّرُ الهَوَاءُ فجأةً
على يدٍ ممدودة
في الظَّلام.
أحدُنا يقولُ: "صباحٌ"
فيرتدُّ غُباراً
على عتبةِ بابٍ يفضي
إلى جدارٍ فحسب.

وجهٌ على كنبةٍ. وجهٌ أمامَ جدار.
في صُورةٍ فُوتُوغرافيَّة.
في نظرة.

أو:
ماذا يفعلُ هذا الوجهُ هنا
حيث لا شيءَ
سوى بياضٍ ضرير
في غُرف نومٍ تقطنُها الوحشـة
أو الرُّطُوبة
أو الصمتُ؟

أو:
وجهٌ ذاهلٌ أمامَ نافذة
تعبرُ به الأشجار
ويظلُّ كذلك، في ذُهُول

We climb rooms to the words
we mistake for doors.
We stand for a long time before the paradox.
One of us says: "A door,"
and suddenly, the air petrifies
around a hand extended
in the dark.
One of us says: "Morning,"
and turns to dust
on the threshold of a door
that leads
only to a wall.

A face on a couch, a face in front of a wall,
in a photograph,
in a glance.

Or:
What is this face doing here
where there is nothing
but white blindness
in bedrooms inhabited
by desolation,
or dampness,
or silence?

Or:
A bewildered face in front of a window
as the trees pass by

لا يطلبُ تفسيراً،
لأنَّ نظرةً واحدة
تكفي لاختصارِ حياة
كانتْ كثيراً
أو لم تكنْ.

شيءٌ لا يصلُ.
كلماتٌ كثيرةٌ تفقدُ ضوءَها
قبلَ أن تُولَد.
الصُّورُ صداعٌ مُقيم
في رأسٍ مُعطَّل
كَحَياة
من نافذةِ قطار
يظلُّ يعبرُ
هذه الغُرفةَ المقفِرة.
رجلٌ بلا نافذة.
بلا سماء.
رجلٌ مع سيجارة.
رجلٌ على مقعد.
أمامَ بحر.

يتحرَّكُ قليلاً
فترتعشُ ستارة،
في حياةٍ أُخرى.

remains in confusion,
asking for no explanation,
because a single glance
is enough to summarize a life
that was too much,
or never was.

Something doesn't arrive.
Many words lose their light
before they are born.
The images are an ache
nestled in a defunct head,
like a life
seen from the window
of a train passing through
this deserted room.
A man without a window,
without a sky.
A man with a cigarette
on a bench
in front of the sea.

He shifts a little.
A curtain rustles
in another life.

Other Poems

لم يَعُدْ مُهمّاً أن يُحبَّنا أحدٌ

لم يَعُدْ مُهمّاً، بعدَ اليوم، أنْ يُحبَّنا أحدٌ
يكفـي أنْ يُحبَّنا الملاكُ العظيمُ
في سمائِهِ النَّاصعة

يـراهُ أطفالُنا واقفاً في البعيد
ضامَّاً يدَيْهِ في رسمِ قلبٍ
فيبتسمُونَ
تراهُ نساؤُنا مُلوِّحاً بياسمينةٍ بيضاءَ
فيُغمِضْنَ عُيُونهنَ مرّةً
وإلى الأبد
يرى رجالُنا أجنحَتَهُ الزَّرقاء
الصَّافيةَ كَسَماء
فتنخطفُ قُلوبُهم
ويشدُّونَ الرِّحالَ إليه

لـم يَعُدْ مُهمّاً أنْ يُحبَّنا أحدٌ
الطَّائراتُ حرَّرتْنا من آذانِنا
التي كنَّا نسمعُ بها كلماتِ الحُبِّ
القذائفُ حرَّرتْنا من عُيُوننا
التي كنَّا نرى بها نظراتِ الحُبِّ
وحرَّرتْنا الكلماتُ السُّـودُ مِن قُلُوبِنا
التي كنَّا نرى فيها تعاويذَ الحُبِّ

لـم يَعُدْ مُهمّاً أن يُحبَّنا أحدٌ
في هذا العالَم
"يبدو، على أيِّ حالٍ، أنَّهُ كان حُبَّاً مِن طرفٍ واحدٍ"

It No Longer Matters If Anyone Loves Us

It no longer matters
if anyone loves us.
The love of the great angel
in his bright white sky
is enough.

Our children see him standing in the distance,
holding his hands in the shape of a heart
and they smile.
Our women see him waving a sprig of white jasmine
and close their eyes once
and forever.
Our men see his blue wings
as clear as a sky.
Their hearts are seized,
and they set out toward him.

It no longer matters
if anyone loves us.
Bombs have liberated us from our ears,
with which we used to hear words of love.
Rockets have liberated us from our eyes,
with which we used to see loving glances.
Hate-filled words have liberated us from our hearts,
in which we used to cherish the enchantments of love.

It no longer matters
if anyone in this world loves us.

يقولُ شُيوخُنا المُتعَبُونَ مِن فكرةِ الأرض
ويقفُ شاعرُنا في الأُفقِ البعيدِ
ويَهتِفُ: "أنقِذُونا مِن هذا الحُبِّ القاسي"،
ثمَّ يَهمِسُ مُعتذراً عن تفاؤُلٍ صبيانيٍّ عابر:
ليسَ على هذه الأرض
ما يستحقُّ الحياة

لـم يَعُدْ مُهمّاً أن يُحبَّنا أحدٌ
تَعِبْنا مِن كلماتٍ تُقالُ ولا تُقالُ
ومِـن أيدٍ تَمتدُّ ولا تَمتدُّ
ومِن عُيُونٍ تَرى ولا تَرى،
تَعِبْنا مِن أنفسِنا
في هذا اللَّيلِ الطَّويل
وتَعِبْنا مِن تشبُّثِ أُمَّهاتِنا
بما بقيَ منَّا
ومِن صخرةٍ نَحملُها على ظُهورِنا
لعنةً أبديَّةً
ونمضي بها مِن هاويةٍ إلى هاوية
ومِن موتٍ لموت
ولا نَصِل

لم يَعُدْ مُهمّاً، بعدَ اليوم، أن يُحبَّنا أحدٌ
ولا أن يُرافِقَنا أحدٌ في جنازةِ أنفسِنا
هـا نحنُ نمضي بصمتٍ إلى تِيْهٍ أخير
نُمسِكُ أيديَ بعضِنا بعضاً
ونتقدَّمُ وحيدينَ في صحراءِ العالَم،
في لحظةٍ ما
يلتفتُ طفلٌ منّا إلى الوراء
يُلقي نظرةً على الرُّكام
ويَذرِفُ دمعةً أخيرة.

"It seems to have been an unreciprocated love, anyway,"
say our elders, now exhausted by the idea of land.
Our poet stands on the distant horizon and proclaims:
"Save us from your cruel love!"
He then whispers, apologizing for an earlier, childish optimism:
"On this Earth,
nothing deserves life."

It no longer matters
if anyone loves us.
We are tired of words, the said and the unsaid,
tired of hands that reach out but do not touch,
of eyes that see but do not see.
We are tired of ourselves in this endless night,
and tired of our mothers clinging to what's left of us,
tired of this rock we carry on our backs,
this eternal curse.
From abyss to abyss, we carry it,
from death to death,
and we never arrive.

It no longer matters, after this, if anyone loves us,
or if anyone walks in our funerals.
Here we go in silence toward the final abyss.
We hold each other's hands,
go forth alone in this desert of a world.
At some moment, one of us, a child, will look back,
will cast one last glance at the ruins, and
shedding a single tear, will say:
"It no longer matters that anyone love us."

أهلي

هناكَ فوقَ أرضٍ - قِيلَ لنا - ليسـتْ أرضَنَا،
تحتَ سماءٍ - قِيلَ لنا - ليستْ سماءَنا
يعيشُ أهلي مَوتَهُم

لا نعرفُ كيف وصلْنا إلى هنا
ولا مكانَ آخرَ نمضي إليه
لكنَّنا، في ذُروَةِ اليأسِ، نُناجي آلهةَ الشَّتَات:
أعِينِيْنا يا آلهة
على فَهْمِ هذه المُعضِلَة،
فنحنُ لا نريدُ أنْ نُوذيَ مشاعرَ الصَّحراء
ولا أنْ نُقلِقَ سُكُونَ الجبل
والمدينةُ كثيرةٌ وشاهقةٌ أسوارُها
فإلى أينَ المسير؟

كنَّا في حديقةٍ لا نعرفُ إنْ كانتْ - هي الأخرى - لنا
ولم تَكُنِ الحديقةَ الأجملَ
إذ لم يَكُنْ فيها شجرٌ ولا ثمرٌ
ولا طُيُورٌ تُعشِّشُ في خرائبِ أرواحِنا
وجَدْنا أنفسَنا هنا ذاتَ يومٍ
وقُلنا هذه حديقَتُنا
وحَفَرْنا جُحُورَنا بالإبَر
واختبَأنا من الشَّمسِ اللَّاهبةِ في ظِلالِ ذكرياتٍ بعيدةٍ
عن حياةٍ قِيلَ لنا إنَّها - هي الأخرى - ليستْ لنا

لم نأتِ مِن جهةٍ ولا مِن مكان
تَساقَطْنا كالغُبارِ مِن نجمةٍ ميتةٍ
بمحضِ مُصادفةٍ فَلَكِيَّةٍ

My People

There, on a land, we were told was not our land,
under a sky, we were told, was not our sky,
my people live their death.

We don't know how we got here,
and there's nowhere else to go.
At the peak of despair,
we implore the gods
of diaspora:
Help us understand this dilemma, we say.
We don't want to hurt the desert's feelings
or disturb the mountain's peace,
and the city walls are high and many.
Where to go, then?

In a garden—not the most beautiful garden,
and who knows whether ours or not,
no trees, no fruit, no birds nesting
in the ruins of our souls
—we found ourselves one day.
Our garden, we said.
We dug our burrows with needles
and hid from the scorching sun
in the shade of distant memories,
the memories of life—we were also told—was not ours.

We did not come from a place or a direction.
We fell like the dust of a dying star,

مِنْ تعامُدِ الشَّمسِ مع كوكبِ اليأسِ؛
لا فكرةَ لدينا عمَّا كانَ في البدايةِ
ولا عمَّا سيكونُ في النِّهاية
لمْ نَعُدْ نَذكُرْ شيئاً
سوى أنَّنا هنا
نتشاطرُ رغيفاً يابساً
وعالَماً يابساً
ودُمُوعَ أنهارٍ جفَّت
وأمَّهات

لا لونَ لنا
ولنا جميعُ الألوان
لا ملامحَ أقسى أو أرقّ
ولا لغةَ
لا نُقطةَ انطلاقٍ
ولا وُجهةً أخيرةً
في كلِّ مطارٍ على هذا الكوكب
واحدٌ منَّا
يصفُ لغريبٍ عِلَّةَ وُجُودِهِ على هذهِ الأرض

نعيشُ حياةً شيِّقة
كلُّ يومٍ مُغامرة
وكلُّ نَفَسٍ مُعجزة
وحينَ نَمُوتُ أخيراً
نَمُوتُ كثيراً
يُضجِرُنا الرَّحيلُ ويُفزِعُنا الشَّتاتُ؛
حَتفُنا جَلَبَةٌ تكفي
ليومٍ شَيِّقٍ آخرَ في أكنافِ السَّماءْ

a mere cosmic coincidence,
the sun aligning with the star of despair.
We have no idea what was in the beginning
nor what will be at the end.
We remember nothing except that
we are here,
sharing a dried-out loaf of bread,
a dried-up world,
and the tears of dry rivers
and mothers.

We have no color
—and all the colors are ours—
no hardened features,
no language,
no launching point,
no final direction.
In every airport on this planet,
one of us describes to a stranger
the malady of our existence on this earth.

We live an exciting life.
Every day is an adventure,
every breath a miracle.
And when we die, finally,
we die a lot.
Bored of displacement,
terrified of diaspora,
our doom is enough racket
for another exciting day
in the bosom of the sky.

لـم يَعِدْنا ربٌّ بشيءٍ، وأهملتْ ذِكرَنا الكُتْبُ
تُركِنا نُطاردُ أشباحاً تُطارِدُنا
من أجلِ مِصعدٍ
لم يَعُدْ يَصعَدُ
إلى أيِّ سماء

أهلي يُدوِّنونَ أسماءَ أطفالِهِمْ على الأيدي والسِّيقان
ليتعرَّفوا عليهم في المَقْتَلَات
يُرسِلُونَ نظَراتِهم بعيداً في الحُقُول
ولا يَنسَـونَ أنْ يتلمَّسُوا في الطُّرُقِ
كلَّ حجرٍ صارخٍ
وكلَّ غُصنٍ مُستحيل
لعلَّ إشارةً أو صوتاً،
لعلَّ أُغنيَّةً أو صلاة
تُعيدُ وَصْلَهم
في ظُلْمَةٍ واحدة.

No god promised us anything,
and the books neglected our names.
We were left to chase ghosts that chase us
to an elevator, out of order,
ascending to the skies.

My people write the names of their children
on arms and legs, so they can find them
later among the massacred.
They cast their gazes far into the fields.
They touch every screaming rock along the way,
every impossible branch,
hoping for a sign or a sound,
a song or a prayer,
to reunite them in the same darkness.

المدينةُ الأخيرةُ
(رُوحُ الرُّوحِ)

في خرائبِ هذه المدينةِ الأخيرة
في هـذا اللَّيلِ الذي هو اللَّيل
بجوارِ سريرِكِ الصَّغير
الذي مزَّقتْهُ الوُحُوش
أقفُ عارياً منِّي
ومِن كلِّ شيء

بهـاتَيْنِ اليدَيْنِ القليلتَيْنِ أحملُكِ
وأضُمُّكِ
إلى أبعـدَ ما يمضي إليه قلبي،
وأرفعُكِ عالياً في الهواء،
وَلَكَمْ خفيفةٌ الآنَ أنتِ، يا صغيرتي
وَلَكَمْ ثقيلٌ هذا الهواءُ
وهذا الجسدُ
الذي كان يوماً لكِ

أحملُكِ ...
أأحملُكِ حقَّاً؟
أيحملُ رجلٌ رُوحَه
مثلما يحملُ قتيلٌ قميصَهُ المُخضَّبَ بالدَّم؟
أيولدُ رجلٌ مِن دُمُوعِه
مثلما تُولَدُ شجرةٌ مِن أوراقِها؟
أيولَدُ جَدٌّ من حفيدتِه
مثلما تُولَدُ ياسمينةٌ مِن عطرِها؟

The Final City
(to the soul of my soul)

In the ruins of this final city,
in this night of nights,
by your small bed
torn apart by monsters,
I stand naked,
stripped of myself
and of everything.

With these scarce hands I cradle you.
I embrace you and lift you up
as far as my heart can reach.
How light you are now, my little one,
and how heavy this air.
How heavy this body
that once belonged to you.

I carry you—
but is this really you?
Can a man carry his soul
as a dead man carries his blood-stained shirt?
Is a man born from his own tears
as a tree is born from its leaves?
Is a grandfather born with his granddaughter
as a jasmine blossom is born with its scent?

أحملُكِ يا صغيرتي
كأنّي أحملُ دفعةً واحدةً كلَّ الحجارةِ الأرواحِ الدِّماءِ الصَّرخاتِ الظِّلالِ الأيَّامِ
الأزمنةِ الميتةِ
والصَّباحاتِ المُجهضَة
كأنّي أحملُ كلَّ الأنهارِ التي جفَّت
في شفتَيْكِ
كلَّ السُّهولِ التي تبدَّدت
في عينَيْكِ
كلَّ الجبالِ التي استحالتْ حَفنةَ غُبار
تحتَ قَدَمَيْكِ اللَّتَيْن لن تطآ بعدَ اليوم
هذه اليابسةَ اليابسة.

عارياً أقفُ بين يدَيْكِ الصَّغيرتَيْن
غارقاً في نعيمِ لمستِكِ الغائبة
مُغتسلاً في ضوءِ عينَيْكِ المغمضتَيْن
كأنَّني الآنَ كلُّ الموتى
كأنَّكِ كلُّ الولادات.

ولا أعرفُ يا صغيرتي
هل أصابَكِ في تلك اللحظةِ ألمٌ؟
هل لمعَ مِن أجلِكِ ضوءٌ في تلكَ السَّماءِ القاحلة؟
هل ضمَّكِ ملاكٌ رحيمٌ؟
هل وضعتْ أمُّكِ راحتَها فوق قلبِكِ
كي لا ينفجرَ قلبُها؟

كأنَّ كلَّ هذا لم يكن
هُنيهاتٍ قليلةً أغيبُ فيها في حليبِ وجنتَيْكِ النَّاصعتَيْن
أذوبُ في تلكَ البقعـةِ الطَّرِيَّةِ عندَ منتصفِ جبينِكِ،

I carry you, my little one,
as if I were carrying the stones,
the souls, the blood, the screams,
the shadows, the days,
the dead epochs,
the aborted mornings
all at once,
as if I were carrying
all the rivers that dried up on your lips,
all the meadows that scattered in your eyes,
all the mountains that turned to dust
under your feet that will never again
touch this scorched land.

I carry you, my little one.
Naked I stand between your little hands,
drowned in the bliss of your absent touch,
drenched in the light on your closed eyes,
as if I were now all the dead,
and you all the newborns.

I wish I knew, little one.
Did you feel pain in the moment?
Did a light flash for you in the barren sky?
Did a merciful angel embrace you?
Did your mother place her palm on your heart
so her own heart would not burst?

As if all this never were . . .
If only I could lose myself
in the milk of your white cheeks.

أذكرُ، حتَّى أمسِ قريب،
كان يكفي أن أمسَّ تلكَ البقعةَ بسبَّابتي مَسَّاً خفيفاً
حتَّى تَغِطِّي في نومٍ عميق،

وَلَكَمْ أخافُ إن لمستُها الآن
أن تظلِّي نائمةً إلى الأبد،
كان يكفي، في ذلك الأمسِ القريب،
أن أقرِّبَ أذُني مِن شـفتَيْكِ الصغيرتَيْن
لأسمعَ الينابيعَ البعيدة
تترقرقُ في نَفَسٍ واحد
كان يكفي أن أضَعَ أنفاسي بجوارِ أنفاسِكِ
لتنهضَ في قلبي
جميعُ العصافيرِ التي خذلتْها الدُّروب
ولم تعد

في الطَّريقِ الطَّويلِ إليكِ
كنتُ أسمعُكِ تنادينَ: "جدِّي"
ولم أفهم
فأنتِ لم تتعلَّمي الكلامَ بعد،
لكنِّي سمعتُ
وكان ما سمعتُ صوتَكِ
وكان صوتُكِ في كلِّ شيء
في الهواءِ الذَّبيح
في أنينِ الأشجار
في عُواءِ الجُدران
في الأيدي المَبتورة
وفي الأقدامِ التي تبحثُ عـن خطواتِها التَّائهةِ تحتَ الأنقاض
كان صوتُكِ الحُلوُ ينادي
وكنتُ ألهثُ في إثرِه

For a few fleeting moments,
if I could melt in that little soft spot between your eyes.
I remember. It feels just like yesterday.
You'd drift into deep sleep
every time I lightly touched that spot.

Now I fear touching it,
lest you remain asleep forever.
It feels just like yesterday,
when all I had to do
was place my ear to your lips
to hear the distant springs
rippling in a single breath.
All I had to do was bring my breath to yours
and all the stray birds that had lost their way in my soul
would awaken.

On the long journey,
I used to hear you calling:
"Grandfather!" I didn't understand,
You hadn't yet learned to speak,
and still I heard you.
It was your voice
and it echoed in everything,
in the slaughtered air,
in the moaning trees,
in the howling on the walls,
in the severed limbs,
in the feet searching for their lost steps amid the rubble.
Your sweet voice called,
and I hurried after it,

"جَدِّي ..."
ولم أعرفْ أَهذا صوتُكِ
أم أصواتُ جميعِ الأطفالِ الضَّائعين
في مَتاهاتِ المَحرَقَة
وبين دُخانٍ ودُخان
كنتُ أرى أَيْدِيَاً صغيرةً داميةً تُلوِّحُ لي
أم لعلَّها ترَبَّتْ رُوحي
أم لعلَّها تُناديني
لكي أخرِجَها مِن جحيمِ تلكَ الغابةِ السَّوداء
في الطَّريقِ الطَّويلِ إليكِ
رأيتُ قوافلَ أهلي الهاربين
أهلي السَّالكينَ دُرْبَ الأهوال
وتذكَّرتُ أبي
كيف حملَني أيَّاماً على كتفَيْهِ المُتعبَتَيْن
وكيف حملتُهُ في قلبي ألفَ عام.

وكلَّما هاجَني شوقٌ إليه
كنتُ أمسِكُ حَفْنَةَ تُرابٍ وألثمُها
وأتعلَّمُ شيئاً جديداً عن الحُبِّ والصَّبر
والألم
وهكذا أيضاً تعلَّمتُ أن أبتسِمَ كلَّما أعياني الكلام،
لأنِّي أعرفُ أن أبي
لا يزال
حيثُ تركتُهُ آخَر مرَّة
وأنَّهُ يبتسمُ لي.

بانكسارِ المُتعبِين
وحنينِ الغائبين
أحملُكِ يا صغيرتي

"Grandfather!"
Was it your voice
or the voices of all the children lost
in the mazes of the massacre?
Between one veil of smoke and another,
I glimpsed small, bloodied hands waving to me.
Perhaps they were comforting me,
perhaps they were calling me
to rescue them from the hell
of that black forest.
On the long journey to you,
I saw the caravans of my fleeing people,
my kin on the paths of disaster.
I remembered my father
and how he bore me for days
on his weary shoulders,
and how I carried him in my heart
for a thousand years.

Whenever longing for him surged within me,
I'd grasp a handful of soil, kiss it,
and learn something new about love,
patience, and anguish.
That's also how I learned to smile
each time words failed me.
For I know that my father remains
where I left him last
and that he is smiling back at me.

With the defeat of the weary
and the longing of the absent,

أضمُّكِ إلى صدري
فتضمِّيني إلى رُوحي
تجمعينَ أشلائي المُتلاشِية
في الأزقَّةِ والأرصفة
تجمعينَ دمِي المَسفُوح
على أطرافِ الأسِنَّة.

تجمعينَ كلماتي الآسنَة
في الكُتُبِ المُغبَّرَة
تجمعينَ صُراخي المُبدَّد
في صحراءِ الأرض
تُلَمْلِمين بقايا أهلي
مِن الحُفَرِ السَّوداء
وتُعيدِينَني كاملاً إليَّ

ها نحنُ الآن هنا
طِفلان يَتيمان وقد غَدَوْنا واحداً
في مَقتَلَة
أنا أحملُ رُوحَكِ
وأنتِ تحملينَ جُثَّتي
على مَشارِفِ هذه المدينة
التي صارتْ حُفرَة
على مَشارِفِ هذه الحُفرَة
التي هي العالَم.

I carry you, my little one.
I embrace you to my chest.
You embrace me into my soul.
You gather my remains
scattered in the alleys and on the sidewalks.
You collect my blood
spilled on the edges of blades.

You gather my words,
stale in the dusty books.
You gather my screams
fading in the deserts of this earth.
You gather the remains of my people
from the dark pits and you restore me
whole to myself.

Here we are now, you and I,
two orphaned children,
having become one
in the massacre.
I carry your soul,
and you carry my corpse,
on the outskirts of this city
that has become an abyss,
on the edge of this abyss
that is the world.

مِن النَّهرِ إلى البحرِ

كلُّ شارعٍ، كلُّ بيتٍ، كلُّ غُرفةٍ، كلُّ نافذةٍ، كلُّ شُرفةٍ، كلُّ جدارٍ، كلُّ حجرٍ، كلُّ شجنٍ، كلُّ كلمةٍ، كلُّ حرفٍ، كلُّ همسةٍ، كلُّ لمسةٍ، كلُّ نظرةٍ، كلُّ قُبْلَةٍ، كلُّ شجرةٍ، كلُّ عُشبةٍ، كلُّ دمعةٍ، كلُّ صرخةٍ، كلُّ هواءٍ، كلُّ رجاءٍ، كلُّ دُعاءٍ، كلُّ سِرٍّ، كلُّ بئرٍ، كلُّ صلاةٍ، كلُّ أغنيَّةٍ، كلُّ مَوَّالٍ، كلُّ كتابٍ، كلُّ ورقةٍ، كلُّ لونٍ، كلُّ شُعاعٍ، كلُّ غيمةٍ، كلُّ مطرٍ، كلُّ قطرة مطرٍ، كلُّ نُقطةِ عَرَقٍ، كلُّ لُثْغَةٍ، كلُّ تَأْتَأَةٍ، كلُّ "يَمَّةٍ"، كلُّ "يَابَا"، كلُّ ظِلٍّ، كلُّ ضوءٍ، كلُّ يدٍ صغيرةٍ رَسَمَتْ في دفترٍ صغيرٍ شجرةً أو شارعاً أو بيتاً أو قلباً أو عائلةً مِن أبٍ وأُمٍّ وأخوةٍ وحيواناتٍ أليفةٍ، كلُّ شوقٍ، كلُّ احتمالٍ، كلُّ رسالةٍ بين عاشقَيْن وصلتْ أم لم تَصِلْ، كلُّ شهقةِ حُبٍّ تبدَّدت في السُّحُبِ البعيدةِ، كلُّ لحظةِ يأسٍ عندَ كلِّ مُنعطفٍ، كلُّ حقيبةِ سفرٍ فوقَ كلِّ خزانةٍ، كلُّ مكتبةٍ، كلُّ رَفٍّ، كلُّ مِئذنةٍ، كلُّ سجَّادةٍ، كلُّ رَنَّةِ جرسِ كلِّ كنيسةٍ، كلُّ مسبحةٍ، كلُّ تسبيحةٍ، كلُّ وُصُولٍ، كلُّ وداعٍ، كلُّ "صباح الخير" كلُّ "الحمد لله"، كلُّ "على راسي"، كلُّ "حلِّ عن سمائي"، كلُّ صخرةٍ، كلُّ موجةٍ، كلُّ حبَّةِ رملٍ، كلُّ تصفيفةِ شَعْرٍ، كلُّ مِرآةٍ، كلُّ نظرةٍ في كلِّ مِرآةٍ، كلُّ قِطٍّ، كلُّ مُواءِ قِطٍّ، كلُّ حمارٍ سعيدٍ، كلُّ نظرةِ حمارٍ حزينةٍ، كلُّ قِدْرٍ، كلُّ بُخارٍ يتصاعدُ مِن كلِّ قِدْرٍ، كلُّ رائحةٍ، كلُّ وعاءٍ، كلُّ طابورٍ مَدرسيٍّ، كلُّ حذاءٍ مَدرسيٍّ، كلُّ رَنَّةِ جرسٍ، كلُّ سَبُّورةٍ، كلُّ طَبْشُورةٍ، كلُّ مِزْيَلَةٍ، كلُّ "مبروك ما إجاكم" كلُّ "العوض بسلامتك"، كلُّ "عين الحسود تبلى بالعَمَى"، كلُّ صورةٍ فُوتُوغرافيَّةٍ، كلُّ مَنْ في كلِّ صورةٍ فُوتُوغرافيَّةٍ، كلُّ "نيَّالك"، كلُّ "اشتقنالك"، كلُّ حبَّةِ قمحٍ في حَوْصَلةِ كلِّ عُصفورٍ، كلُّ خُصْلَةِ شَعْرٍ، كلُّ ربطةِ شَعْرٍ، كلُّ يدٍ، كلُّ قَدَمٍ، كلُّ كرةِ قَدَمٍ، كلُّ أصبعٍ، كلُّ ظُفرٍ، كلُّ درَّاجةٍ هوائيَّةٍ، كلُّ راكبٍ على كلِّ درَّاجةٍ هوائيَّةٍ، كلُّ هواءٍ في كلِّ درَّاجةٍ هوائيَّةٍ، كلُّ مزحةٍ سخيفةٍ، كلُّ مزحةٍ مَريرةٍ، كلُّ ضحكةٍ، كلُّ ابتسامةٍ، كلُّ شتيمةٍ،

From the River to the Sea

every street, every house, every room, every window, every balcony, every wall, every stone, every sorrow, every word, every letter, every whisper, every touch, every glance, every kiss, every tree, every blade of grass, every tear, every scream, every air, every hope, every supplication, every secret, every well, every prayer, every song, every ballad, every book, every paper, every color, every ray, every cloud, every rain, every drop of rain, every drip of sweat, every lisp, every stutter, every *yamma*, every *yaba*, every shadow, every light, every little hand that drew in a little notebook a tree or house or heart or a family with a father, a mother, siblings, and pets, every longing, every possibility, every letter between two lovers that arrived or didn't arrive, every gasp of love dispersed in the distant clouds, every moment of despair at every turn, every suitcase on top of every closet, every library, every shelf, every minaret, every rug, every bell toll in every church, every rosary, every holy praise, every arrival, every goodbye, every Good Morning, every Thank God, every ala rasi, every hill an samai, every rock, every wave, every grain of sand, every hair-do, every mirror, every glance in every mirror, every cat, every meow, every happy donkey, every sad donkey's gaze, every pot, every vapor rising from every pot, every scent, every bowl, every school queue, every pair of school shoes, every ring of the bell, every blackboard, every piece of chalk, every school costume, every mabruk ma ijakum, every yawid bi-salamtak, every ayn al- ḥasud tibla bil-ama, every photograph, every person in every photograph, every niyyalak, every ishta'nalak, every grain of wheat in every bird's gullet, every lock of hair, every hair knot, every hand, every foot, every football, every finger, every nail, every bicycle, every rider on every bicycle,

كلُّ لهفةٍ، كلُّ شِجارٍ، كلُّ "سِتّي"، كلُّ "سِيْدي"، كلُّ حقلٍ، كلُّ زهرةٍ، كلُّ شجرةٍ، كلُّ بَيَّارةٍ، كلُّ زيتونةٍ، كلُّ برتقالةٍ، كلُّ وردةٍ اصطناعيَّةٍ يَعلُوها غبارٌ على منضدةٍ مهجورةٍ، كلُّ صُورةِ شهيدٍ مُعلَّقةٍ منذُ دهرٍ على جدارٍ، كلُّ شاهدةِ قبرٍ، كلُّ سورةٍ، كلُّ آيةٍ، كلُّ ترتيلةٍ، كلُّ ترنيمةٍ، كلُّ "حجّ مبرور وسعي مشكور"، كلُّ "يلّا تنام يلّا تنام"، كلُّ دبدوبٍ أحمرَ في كلِّ عيدِ حُبٍّ، كلُّ حَبْلِ غسيلٍ، كلُّ تنُّورةٍ مُشتهاةٍ، كلُّ فستانٍ يصنعُ البهجةَ، كلُّ بنطالٍ ممزَّقٍ، كلُّ كنزةٍ تَغزِلُ الأَيَّامَ، كلُّ زرٍّ، كلُّ مِسْمَارٍ، كلُّ أُغنيَّةٍ، كلُّ مَوَّالٍ، كلُّ مِرآةٍ، كلُّ مِشجَبٍ، كلُّ مَقعَدٍ، كلُّ رَفٍّ، كلُّ حُلْمٍ، كلُّ وَهْمٍ، كلُّ أملٍ، كلُّ خيبةٍ، كلُّ يدٍ تَحضُنْ يداً، كلُّ يدٍ وحيدةٍ، كلُّ فكرةٍ شاردةٍ، كلُّ فكرةٍ جميلةٍ، كلُّ فكرةٍ مُفزعةٍ، كلُّ همسةٍ، كلُّ لمسةٍ، كلُّ شارعٍ، كلُّ بيتٍ، كلُّ غُرفةٍ، كلُّ شُرفةٍ، كلُّ عينٍ، كلُّ نظرةٍ، كلُّ دمعةٍ، كلُّ كلمةٍ، كلُّ حرفٍ، كلُّ اسمٍ، كلُّ صوتٍ، كلُّ اسمٍ، كلُّ بيتٍ، كلُّ اسمٍ، كلُّ وجهٍ، كلُّ اسمٍ، كلُّ غيمةٍ، كلُّ اسمٍ، كلُّ وردةٍ، كلُّ اسمٍ، كلُّ عُشبةٍ، كلُّ اسمٍ، كلُّ موجةٍ، كلُّ حبَّةِ رملٍ، كلُّ شجرةٍ، كلُّ قُبْلَةٍ، كلُّ صُورةٍ، كلُّ عينٍ، كلُّ دمعةٍ، كلُّ "يَمَّةً"، كلُّ "يَابَا"، كلُّ اسمٍ، كلُّ اسمٍ، كلُّ اسمٍ، كلُّ اسمٍ، كلُّ اسمٍ، كلُّ اسمٍ، كلُّ ...

every puff of air whirling from every bicycle, every bad joke, every mean joke, every laugh, every smile, every curse, every yearning, every fight, every sitti, every sidi, every meadow, every flower, every tree, every grove, every olive, every orange, every plastic rose covered with dust on an abandoned counter, every portrait of a martyr hanging on a wall since forever, every gravestone, every sura, every verse, every hymn, every ḥajj mabrur wa sayy mashkur, every yalla tnam yalla tnam, every red teddy bear on every Valentine's, every clothesline, every hot skirt, every joyful dress, every torn trousers, every days-spun sweater, every button, every nail, every song, every ballad, every mirror, every peg, every bench, every shelf, every dream, every illusion, every hope, every disappointment, every hand holding another hand, every hand alone, every scattered thought, every beautiful thought, every terrifying thought, every whisper, every touch, every street, every house, every room, every balcony, every eye, every tear, every word, every letter, every name, every voice, every name, every house, every name, every face, every name, every cloud, every name, every rose, every name, every spear of grass, every name, every wave, every grain of sand, every street, every kiss, every image, every eye, every tear, every yamma, every yaba, every name, every name, every name, every name, every name, every name, every name, every name . . .

سوف نخسرُ هذه الحرب

لن نقطعَ شجرة
لن نُحرقَ حقلاً
لن نقتلَ رجلاً ولا امرأةً
شيخاً ولا طفلاً
لن نُقلقَ نومَ جنينٍ
ما زالَ يسبحُ، غافلاً،
في نعيمِ مياهِهِ الأولى
لن نُجفلَ عصفوراً يحلّقُ ساهماً
بين غصنينِ
لـن نعكّر صفو فرسٍ في جريانها الحالمِ
نحو الغروبِ
لـن نُشتّتَ انتباهَ غيمةٍ تعبرُ القرى
لتُذكّرَها بأسمائها الأولى.

سوف نخسرُ هذه الحرب
سوف نخسرُ هذه الحرب

بدمائنا المسفوكةِ
سوف نخسرُ هذه الحربَ
بأطرافنا المبتورةِ
سوف نخسرُ هذه الحربَ
بعيوننا المثلومةِ
وقلوبنا المكلومةِ
وأنّاتنا المفجوعةِ
بالحزنَ الذي يأبى أن يفارقنا
والأسى الذي رعيناه طويلاً

We Will Lose This War

We won't cut down a tree.
We won't burn a field.
We won't kill a man or a woman,
a grandparent or a child.
We won't disturb the sleep of an unborn baby
still swimming, unaware,
in the bliss of first waters.
We won't startle a bird flitting aimlessly
from branch to branch,
or hold back a mare trotting dreamily toward sunset.
We won't distract a cloud passing over villages,
reminding them of their original names.

We will lose this war.
We will lose it

with our spilled blood.
We will lose it
with our severed limbs,
our gouged eyes,
our wounded hearts.
We will lose the war
with our bereft howls,
with a sorrow that refuses to leave us,
a grief we've been tending for so long
it has become our twin, our loyal shadow.

حتى صارَ توأمنا وظلنا الدائم
سوف نخسرُ
ثم سوف نخسرُ هذه الحربَ.

سوف نخسرُ هذه الحربَ
مثلما خسرنا كلّ حربٍ جاءتْ قبلها
وكلّ حربٍ ستأتي بعدها
سوف نخسرُ الحربَ
حين نتذكرُ كلّ ما جرى
وحين ننسى كلّ ما جرى
وحين لا نتذكرُ ولا ننسى
وحين نصيرُ محضَ هباءٍ في الرّيحِ
وصدى هائماً في الفلاةِ
سوف نخسرُ الحربَ
مرةً أخرى.

لكننا
وقبل أن نخسرَ الحربَ
وبعد أن نخسرَ الحربَ
سنظلّ نُحدّقُ في عيونِ قاتلنا
سننشبُ نظراتنا في روحِهِ
سنقيمُ في كوابيسِهِ
سننامُ في سريرهِ
سنجلسُ إلى مائدتهِ
سنكونُ قهوتهُ في الصباحِ
ونبيذهُ في المساءِ.

وحين يقفُ خلفَ النافذةِ
لن يراهُ الطائرُ
لأنهُ سيكونُ منكبّاً على جَمعِ شتاتنا

We will lose this war
and then lose it again.

We will lose this war
the way we lost each war before it
and every one after.
We will lose the war
when we remember everything that happened,
when we forget everything that happened,
and when we neither remember nor forget.
And finally as mere dust in the wind,
a wandering echo in the wilderness,
we will, once again,
lose the war.

But
before we lose the war
and after we lose the war,
we will continue to stare into our killers' eyes.
We will anchor our gaze in their souls.
We will live on in their nightmares.
We will sleep in their beds.
We will sit at their tables.
We will be their morning coffee
and their evening wine.

When they look out of windows,
the birds will not see them.
The birds, too devoted to gathering our remains
scattered in the air, will not see them.
When they step into gardens,

في الهواءِ
وحين يخرجُ إلى الحديقةِ
لن تراهُ الشجرةُ
لأنها ستكونُ مشغولةً بحراسةِ أرواحنا الهائمةِ
وحين ينظرُ إلى وجههِ في المرآةِ
لن يرى وجهَهُ
بل سيرانا كُثراً في الضبابِ
وسيعرفُ أخيراً أنه لم يَعُدْ سوى ذكرى شبحٍ
في التيهِ العظيمِ
ولن يفهمَ يوماً: كيف أنه أبادنا
ثم أبادنا
ثم أبادنا
ولم يستطعْ أن يمحوَ من مرآتهِ
صورتنا الساطعة
ولا أن يمحوَ من وجوهنا
ذلك الضوء الذاهل
وتلك الابتسامة الناصعة.

the trees, too busy guarding our wandering souls,
will not see them either.

When our killers look into mirrors,
they will not see their faces,
but ours, many of us, in the mist.

They will finally realize that they have become nothing
but memories of ghosts in the great abyss.

They will never understand how they annihilated us
then annihilated us,
then annihilated us,
and yet could not erase from their mirrors
our shining image
nor could they erase from our faces
that hazy, oblivious light,
that pure, radiant smile.

عُلبةُ تَمرٍ على طاولةِ المَطْبَخ

على طَاولةِ المَطْبَخ، مَا بَقيَ مِنْ حَبّاتِ تَمرٍ في العُلبةِ
لا أَعْرفُ لِمَاذَا ما زلنا نَحتفظُ بها
هُنا حَيـثُ نَراها كلَّ صباحٍ ونحنُ نُعدُّ قهوتنا
وَكلَّ ظـهيرةٍ وَنحنُ نُعدُّ الغداءَ،
وَكُلما دَخَلنا لِجلبِ كُوبِ مَاءٍ، أو كُلما
أرَدْنا أنْ نَراهَا ولا نَراها
هُنا، بَيْنَ أشياءَ أُخرى تَحْجبُها حِيناً
وَتُبْدِيْهَا حِيناً سَاطِعَةً في الظلام

لَمْ تَكُنْ دَوْماً هنا؛
قَبْـلَ بِضْعَةِ أيّام، كَانَتْ على طَاولةٍ أُخرى
في المتجرِ العَرَبيِّ الوَحيدِ في هذه المَدينة
حَيـثُ فَاتتنا رؤيةُ كُلِّ شَيءٍ،
فاتتنا رؤيةُ العَلامَةِ - "الملك داود"- أعلى العُلبَةِ،
مع النّجمَةِ واسمِ المُسْتَعمَرةِ على ظَهْرِها –
وأسمَعُ الآنَ أصواتَ العَالمينَ بالمَسائلِ والأُمورِ:
أوَلَمْ تَتَعلَّم ألفَ بَاءِ المُقَاطَعةِ، أنْ تَقرأَ جيّداً
مـا دُوّنَ على ظَهْرِ العُلبةِ،
أنْ تَبحثَ عن الرّموزِ والإشَارَاتِ الخَفيّةِ والظّاهرةِ،
أنْ تُفكّكَ شِيفرَةَ المُنتجَاتِ،
أوَلَمْ تُشَاوِرْ ما جَاءَ في القَائمةِ؟

أنظرُ إلى حَبيبتي، وَأقولُ:
لكنّها، في نهايةِ الأمرِ، تَبْقَى لنا،
كُلُّ حَبّةِ تَمرٍ في هذه العُلبةِ
وَفي كُلِّ العُلبِ،
هي في الأصلِ لنا،

A Box of Dates on the Kitchen Table

On the kitchen table
is what's left of dates in a box.
I don't know why we keep it still,
there for us to see every morning,
when we make our coffee,
every noon while we prepare lunch,
every time we go to get a glass of water,
every time we want to see it and every time we don't,
there it stands among other things, sometimes hidden
and sometimes revealed, gleaming in the dark.

The box was not always here.
A few days ago, it was on another table
in the only Arab shop in this city.
And it was there that we missed everything.
We missed the brand name, "King David," on the box,
the star and the name of the settlement on the back.
I can hear the pontificators now:
"Don't you know the ABCs of boycott.
Carefully read the back side.
Look for the symbols and signs, the hidden and the visible.
Decode everything on the product.
Did you consult the list?"

I look at my beloved and say:
"But aren't these dates ours at the end of the day?
Each one of them in this box

التربةُ، حيثُ نَبَتَتْ، لنا
والمياهُ التي رَوَتْها،
والظّلالُ التي صَنَعتها،
وَرُبّما حتى الأيدي التي رَعَتْها
هي الأخرى لنا
"إلا الأيدي"، تَقولُ حبيبتي، "إنّها الحقيقةُ الواضحةُ"،
إذنْ لنا ذاكِرَةُ الأيْدي، أقولُ،
الأيدي التي كَانَتْ تُرَبّتُ، وَتَحنو، وَتُحبّ
وَتَحفرُ عَرَقها في النّسْغِ والجِذْعِ والسّعْفةِ
الأيدي التي هي السّعْفَةُ
في تَلويحَتِها الأبَديّةِ للرّاحِلين

في البَيتِ، أقِفُ وَحَبيبتي حَائرَينِ حَوْلَ العُلبةِ
كَأنّما حَوْلَ جُثّةِ حَيَوانٍ نَافِقٍ،
أقولُ لها: إنّها عُلْبَةٌ، مُجَرّدُ عُلْبَةٍ سَخيفةٍ بَائِسةٍ،
غِلافٌ لا أكثَرَ، عَلامَةٌ تِجارِيّةٌ، اسْمٌ مُصْطَنَعٌ، لَوْحَةٌ إعلانيّةٌ،
أوَلَمْ تَرَيْ يا حبيبتي كَمْ تكذِبُ الأسْماءُ المُصْطَنَعَةُ وَاللوحاتُ الإعلانيّةُ؟
أوَلَمْ تَرَيْ كَمْ تَخدَعُ العُلَبُ؟
"بَيْدَ أنّ هذه العُلبةَ صَارَتْ بَلَداً"، تَقولُ
"لكنّهُ ليسَ بَلَداً حَقّاً"، أقولُ، "إنّهُ مُجَرّدُ عُلْبَةٍ أُخرى، اسْمٌ مُصْطَنَعٌ،
عَلامَـةٌ تِجاريّةٌ، ثمَ أوَلَمْ تَرَي تَارِيخَ الصَّلاحيّةِ
على ظَهْرِ العُلْبَةِ؟

وحيداً في المَسَاءِ أنظُرُ إلى العُلْبَةِ المَهجورَةِ على الطّاوِلَةِ،
العُلْبَةُ التي صَارَتْ قبراً ما زالَ يَتّسِعُ
وأذكّرُ نَفسي: إنّها مُجَرّدُ عُلْبَةٍ، عُلْبَةٍ سَخيفةٍ بَائِسةٍ،
فيا نَخْلاتِ أريحا
وَيا نَخْلاتِ خان يونس

and in all the other boxes?
Aren't they all ours to begin with,
the soil where they grew, ours,
the water that nourishes them, ours,
the shade they make, ours.
Maybe even those hands that grew them,
those are probably ours too."
"All but those hands," my beloved says, "that is an obvious truth."
"But ours is the memory of the hands," I say,
"the hands that used to care and nurture and love,
the hands that bled their sweat into the sap, the trunk, the frond—
the hands that are that palm leaf
eternally waving to those departed."

At home, I stand with my beloved,
puzzled over the box,
as if it were a dead animal.
I tell her: "It's just a box, a silly, miserable box,
nothing more than wrapping and a brand,
a made-up name, an advertisement.
Don't you know, my love, that made-up names and ads
are nothing but lies? You know how deceiving a box can be."
"But this box has become a country," she says.
"It's not really a country," I say, "It's just another box, a made-up
    name, a brand.
Besides, didn't you see the expiration date
on the back of the box?"
Alone in the evening, I stare at the box abandoned on the table,
the box that became a grave, now expanding.

وَيا نَخْلاتِ دير البلح
أَتَرَيْنَني وأنا أُمَزِّقُ العُلْبَةَ وأرميها في سَلَّةِ القُمَامَةِ
ثمّ كَيْفَ تَكْبُرُ السَلةُ أكْثَرَ فأَكْثَر
حَتّى تَصيرَ تَتَّسِعُ لكُلّ العُلَبِ في كُلّ المَتَاجِر، في كُلّ المدن،
حَتّى لا يَبْقى سِوى حَبَّةِ تَمْرٍ واحِدَةٍ
أنْزَعُ عَنها قِشْرَتَها الشّاحِبَةَ المَيتةَ
وَأكشِفُ عن الحَجَرِ اللامِعِ في قَلْبِهَا

وَفي الحَجَرِ أرَى كُلَّ شَيءٍ:
مَاضيَ الأشياءِ وَحاضرَها وَمُستقبلها،
البيوتَ وَالحقولَ وَالغيْمَ وَالموجَ
وَكُلَّ مَا نُسمّيه البلادَ،
ثمّ أنزَعُ عن الحَجَرِ ما انْتُحِلَ لهُ من أسمَاء
على دُرُوبِ الغِيَابِ الطويلَةِ،
وَأُعيْدهُ إلى اسمِهِ الأوّلِ
وَأُعيْدُ قلبي إليْه.

I remind myself: it's just a box, a silly, miserable box.
O Palm trees of Jericho,
Palm trees of Khan Younis, of Deir al-Balah,
do you see me as I tear up the box and throw it in the trash bin?
Do you see how the trash bin keeps growing larger and larger,
until it can hold all the boxes from all the stores, in all the cities,
until nothing remains but a single date.
I peel off its pale, lifeless skin,
and reveal the gleaming stone at its heart.

And in the stone, I see all things,
past, present, and future:
the houses, the fields, the clouds, the waves,
all that we call home.
I will strip the stone of all the false names
imposed on it along the endless paths of absence.
I will return it to its first name—
and return it to my heart.

Samer Abu Hawwash is a Palestinian poet, novelist, editor, and translator, born in Lebanon. He is the author of 10 poetry collections including his debut collection *Life is Printed in New York* (1997), *I'll Kill You Death* (2012), *One Last Selfie with a Dying World* (2015), *Ruins* (2020), and *From the River to the Sea* (2024). He is also the author of three works of fiction: *The Journal of Photographed Niceties* (2003), *Valentine's Day* (2005), and *Happiness or A Series of Explosions that Rocked the Capital* (2007). Abu Hawwash is the translator of more than 20 volumes of poetry and prose from English including works by William Faulkner, J.G. Ballard, Sylvia Plath, Charles Bukowski, Langston Hughes, Jack Kerouac, Yann Martel, Hanif Kureishi, Denis Johnson, Marilynne Robinson, and many others. He lives in Barcelona, Spain where he currently works as the director of the Culture & Society section at *Almajalla Magazine*.

Huda J. Fakhreddine is a writer, translator, and Associate Professor of Arabic Literature at the University of Pennsylvania. She is the author of *Metapoesis in the Arabic Tradition* (Brill) and *The Arabic Prose Poem: Poetic Theory and Practice* (Edinburgh University Press), and the co-editor of *The Routledge Handbook of Arabic Poetry* (Routledge). Her translations include Jawdat Fakhreddine's poetry collection *Lighthouse for the Drowning* (BOA Editions), *The Universe, All at Once: Selections from Salim Barakat* (Seagull Books), and *Palestinian: Four Poems* by Ibrahim Nasrallah (World Poetry). She is also the author of a book of creative nonfiction, *Zaman saghīr taḥt shams thāniya* (A Brief Time Under a Different Sun) and a poetry collection, *Wa min thamma al-ālam* (And Then the World). She is co-editor of *Middle Eastern Literatures*.

This book was typeset in Nassim, a multi-script typeface family designed by Titus Nemeth for Rosetta Type Foundry, Brno. The cover features a detail of a painting by Palestinian artist Bashar Alhroub. Cover design by Andrew Bourne. Typesetting by Don't Look Now. Printed and bound in Lithuania by BALTO Print. Manufactured by Arctic Paper in Sweden, the paper in this book meets EU Ecolabel, Forest Stewardship Council, and Cradle to Cradle certification standards.

 WORLD POETRY

Samer Abu Hawwash
Ruins and Other Poems
tr. Huda J. Fakhreddine

Marie-Noëlle Agniau
The Escapades
tr. Jesse Hover Amar

Nadia Anjuman
*Smoke Drifts:
Selected Poems*
tr. Diana Arterian
& Marina Omar

Jean-Paul Auxeméry
Selected Poems
tr. Nathaniel Tarn

Leire Bilbao
Fish Scales: Selected Poems
tr. Joana Urtasun

Boethius
*The Poems from On the
Consolation of Philosophy*
tr. Peter Glassgold

Maria Borio
Transparencies
tr. Danielle Pieratti

Astrid Cabral
Spotlight on the Word
tr. Alexis Levitin

Jeannette L. Clariond
Goddesses of Water
tr. Samantha Schnee

Jacques Darras
*John Scotus Eriugena
at Laon*
tr. Richard Sieburth

Mario dell'Arco
*Day Lasts Forever:
Selected Poems*
tr. Marc Alan Di Martino

Marie de Quatrebarbes
The Vitals
tr. Aiden Farrell

Ricardo Domeneck
*First Epistle to the
Amphibians: Selected Poems*
tr. by Chris Daniels

Olivia Elias
Chaos, Crossing
tr. Kareem James Abu-Zeid

Gastón Fernández
Apparent Breviary
tr. KM Cascia

Jerzy Ficowski
Everything I Don't Know
tr. Jennifer Grotz
& Piotr Sommer
PEN AWARD FOR POETRY IN TRANSLATION

Antonio Gamoneda
Book of the Cold
tr. Katherine M. Hedeen &
Víctor Rodríguez Núñez

Mireille Gansel
Soul House
tr. Joan Seliger Sidney

Óscar García Sierra
Houston, I'm the problem
tr. Carmen Yus Quintero

Phoebe Giannisi
Homerica
tr. Brian Sneeden

Zuzanna Ginczanka
On Centaurs & Other Poems
tr. Alex Braslavsky

Julien Gracq
Abounding Freedom
tr. Alice Yang

Karmelo C. Iribarren
*You've Heard This One
Before: Selected Poems*
tr. John R. Sesgo

Leeladhar Jagoori
*What of the Earth
Was Saved*
tr. Matt Reeck

*Nakedness Is My End:
Poems from the Greek
Anthology*
tr. Edmund Keeley

Birhan Keskin
*Earthly Conditions:
Selected Poems*
tr. Öykü Tekten

Jazra Khaleed
The Light That Burns Us
ed. Karen Van Dyck

Judith Kiros
O
tr. Kira Josefsson

Dimitra Kotoula
*The Slow Horizon
That Breathes*
tr. Maria Nazos

Maria Laina
Hers
tr. Karen Van Dyck

Maria Laina
Rose Fear
tr. Sarah McCann

Perrin Langda
*A Few Microseconds on
Earth*
tr. Pauline Levy Valensi

Anna Malihon
Girl with a Bullet
tr. Olena Jennings

Afrizal Malna
*Document Shredding
Museum*
tr. Daniel Owen

Joyce Mansour
*In the Glittering Maw:
Selected Poems*
tr. C. Francis Fisher

Manuel Maples Arce
Stridentist Poems
tr. KM Cascia

Selma Meerbaum-Eisinger
Blütenlese
tr. Carlie Hoffman

Ennio Moltedo
Night
tr. Marguerite Feitlowitz

Meret Oppenheim
The Loveliest Vowel Empties:
Collected Poems
tr. Kathleen Heil

Giovanni Pascoli
Last Dream
tr. Geoffrey Brock
RAIZISS/DE PALCHI
TRANSLATION AWARD

Gabriel Pomerand
Saint Ghetto of the Loans
tr. Michael Kasper &
Bhamati Viswanathan

Liliana Ponce
Theory of the Voice and Dream
tr. Michael Martin Shea

Rainer Maria Rilke
Where the Paths Do Not Go
tr. Burton Pike

Amelia Rosselli
Document
tr. Roberta Antognini
& Deborah Woodard

Elisabeth Rynell
Night Talks
tr. Rika Lesser

Waly Salomão
Border Fare
tr. Maryam Monalisa Gharavi

George Sarantaris
Abyss and Song:
Selected Poems
tr. Pria Louka

George Seferis
Book of Exercises II
tr. Jennifer R. Kellogg
ELIZABETH CONSTANTINIDES
MEMORIAL TRANSLATION PRIZE

Seo Jung Hak
The Cheapest France
in Town
tr. Megan Sungyoon

Ahmad Shamlou
Elegies of the Earth:
Selected Poems
tr. Niloufar Talebi

Edith Södergran
Modern Woman
tr. CD Eskilson

Ardengo Soffici
Simultaneities &
Lyric Chemisms
tr. Olivia E. Sears

Liesl Ujvary
Good & Safe
tr. Ann Cotten &
Anna-Isabella Dinwoodie

Paul Verlaine
Before Wisdom:
The Early Poems
tr. Keith Waldrop
& K.A. Hays

Haris Vlavianos
Renaissance
tr. Patricia Barbeito

Witold Wirpsza
Apotheosis of Music
tr. Frank L. Vigoda

Uljana Wolf
kochanie, today i bought bread
tr. Greg Nissan

Ye Lijun
My Mountain Country
tr. Fiona Sze-Lorrain

Verónica Zondek
Cold Fire
tr. Katherine Silver